STAYING POWER

STAYING POWER

On Queerness, Inheritances, and the Families We Choose

ZENA SHARMAN

ARSENAL PULP PRESS
VANCOUVER

STAYING POWER

ARSENAL PULP PRESS
Suite 202 – 211 East Georgia St.
Vancouver, BC V6A 1Z6
Canada
arsenalpulp.com

The publisher gratefully acknowledges the support of the Canada Council for the Arts and the British Columbia Arts Council for its publishing program and the Government of Canada and the Government of British Columbia (through the Book Publishing Tax Credit Program) for its publishing activities.

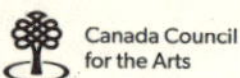

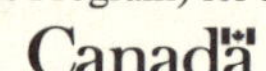

Arsenal Pulp Press acknowledges the xʷməθkʷəy̓əm (Musqueam), Sḵwx̱wú7mesh (Squamish), and səlilwətaɬ (Tsleil-Waututh) Nations, custodians of the traditional, ancestral, and unceded territories where our office is located. We pay respect to their histories, traditions, and continuous living cultures and commit to accountability, respectful relations, and friendship.

Arsenal Pulp Press is committed to reducing the consumption of nonrenewable resources in the making of our books wherever possible. We make every effort to use materials that support a sustainable future. This book is printed on paper made with 100 percent sustainable recycled fibre content.

EU Safety Regulations authorized representative: Easy Access System Europe, Mustamäe tee 50, 10621 Tallinn, Estonia, gpsr.requests@easproject.com.

Cover and text design by Rebecca Poulin
Cover art by Rebecca Poulin
Photo on page 5 courtesy of the author
Edited by Catharine Chen
Proofread by Alison Strobel

Printed and bound in Canada

Library and Archives Canada Cataloguing in Publication:
Title: Staying power : on queerness, inheritances, and the families we choose / Zena Sharman.
Names: Sharman, Zena, 1979– author
Identifiers: Canadiana (print) 20250153777 | Canadiana (ebook) 20250156016 |
ISBN 9781834050164 (softcover) | ISBN 9781834050171 (EPUB)
Subjects: LCSH: Sharman, Zena, 1979– Family. | LCSH: Sexual minority parents. |
LCSH: Sexual minorities' families. | LCSH: Parenthood. |
LCSH: Parent and child. | LCSH: Child rearing. | LCGFT: Essays.
Classification: LCC HQ73.6 .S53 2026 | DDC 306.85086/6—dc23

you cannot move past the grief; the grief must move
through you.
the grief must sting, settle, sediment, sunder, before it can
mother you.

—Jody Chan, “the garden where our future grows”

CONTENTS

Note to Readers 11

The Trauma Archive 15

Thirty-Nine Stages of Grief 37

After Wife 63

Between Worlds 83

Learning to Stay 109

Best Interests of the Child 129

Dolly, Doralee, My Mother, and Me 153

(M)other 171

Love Me Back to Life 193

Acknowledgments 210

Notes 212

NOTE TO READERS

This book took ten years of grieving to write.

When my mother died in 2014, I searched for memoirs that would make me feel less alone. Most of the books I found only increased my sense of isolation. I felt too weird, too queer, too messy, too grew-up-poor-with-a-beloved-complicated-crazy-brilliant-mom to see myself in their straight suburban stories. Ariel Gore's memoir, *The End of Eve*, was a lifeline.

Fast-forward to 2025, when a friend who read a draft of this book told me I had written the book they needed when their mom died. *Oh*, I realized. *I wrote the book I needed when my mom died too.*

This book is for my past self, and also for you.

Staying Power is my fourth book and my first memoir. After three anthologies, I'm ready to put more of myself on the page. It's my most honest and personal book (and the horniest). I've challenged myself to write truer and with more courage at every turn. This has asked me to reckon with my past selves as well as who I am in the present, and to see my mother as a fuller and more complex person than I was able to when she was alive.

My mother was a memory keeper, an artist, an activist, and a parent who loved and protected me as ferociously as a mother could. She was a survivor whose history lives under my skin. Her mothering was a scythe she used to sever cycles of intergenerational trauma. I carry her blade in me too. These are my inheritances, just as this book is an artifact I will someday pass down to my three children. I hope they see it as the love letter it is, to them and our family, to the grandmother they never met, and to the queer lineages and histories of defiance that make our family possible.

This is a book about the families we are born into and the families we choose—not the neat-and-tidy nuclear kind, but the sprawling, expansive, forever-in-process queer ones. It's about an everyday practice of interdependence and how, after years of running, I'm learning to stay. I'm grateful to my family for trusting me to tell this story. I have chosen to use pseudonyms for most of the people in this book as the smallest of shields against the spotlight's glare. It's no small thing to love a memoirist, especially at a time when telling queer stories in public feels riskier. I write for the same reason I read: because these stories are essential to our survival, resistance, and ability to imagine the future. They are where we see ourselves and who we could become.

Please read with care, as *Staying Power* touches on some sensitive topics, including grief and death, suicidal ideation and attempts, childhood sexual abuse, ritual abuse, mind control experimentation, intimate partner violence, and stillbirth. I also write about BDSM, including age play and piercing. There are no detailed depictions of abuse or violence. I have endeavoured to bring an ethic of care and dignity to every page of this book and to tell the truth as I know it without making a spectacle of my or anyone else's trauma.

My mother told the truth, and it cost her a family. By doing so, she made it possible for me to grow up safer than she did, and my children safer still. Her love and courage are foundational to who I am. Her death and the series of losses that followed it were my initiation into grief. I came out the other side transformed and found a family of my own, one more expansive than I ever could have imagined. If only my mother had lived to see it.

Thank you for bearing witness to this story. May you find what you need in its pages.

THE TRAUMA ARCHIVE

Some people inherit money or valuables. I inherited an archive my mother spent decades assembling. Then I destroyed it.

I called it her "trauma archive." It consisted of more than two hundred boxes filled with papers, legal documents, newspaper and magazine clippings, videos, and photographs. The boxes had handwritten labels. I can picture my mother, black permanent marker in one hand, menthol cigarette in the other, carefully labelling each one in her familiar rounded printing: "Pedophiles," "Pinochet," "Pit Bulls."

My mother began recovering memories of incest when she was in her thirties and I was an infant. By the time I was in elementary school, she had surfaced memories of surviving ritual abuse and Cold War–era medical experimentation. Her archive told a graphic story of the abuse and torture she suffered as a girl and young woman.

I'm not sure who she made it for. Did she hope I would become her memory keeper? I didn't want to look at what she left behind, let alone make it mine.

My mother was outspoken about her history. I like to think that I inherited her bravery, but I have spent years writing around the edges of these truths because they scare me. I don't talk about what happened to my mother because I'm afraid her story is too much for you. I don't talk about what happened to my mother because I'm afraid you won't believe me.

My childhood had two phases: before my mother remembered what happened to her, and after. Before, we were part of a family; after, we were exiled. When I was seven, we moved to a new city far from my grandparents, with whom we'd previously had a close relationship. My mother needed 1,500 kilometres between herself and our relatives to tell the truth. They retaliated by calling her crazy and a liar. "Please think about leaving the cult of phantom abuse survivors and have a real life," my aunt wrote to my mother in 1993. "I wish that you would give up this garbage and come back to reality."

My aunt was at the hospital when I was born. She and my mother were best friends once. Her first name is my middle name. It doesn't feel like mine. When I see it on my passport or my driver's licence, it reminds me of the rupture at the heart of our family. I will never forget how they punished my mother for remembering.

My mother maintained a fragile peace with her mum, my grandmother, and found new kinship in a community of survivors. Her friends would stop by to smoke and drink coffee at our kitchen table. She kept in touch by phone or mail with those who lived far away. Between costly long-distance calls and collect calls from incarcerated survivors, our phone would sometimes get cut off when the bills were too high. When we got our first computer, she moved much of her correspondence to email. She wouldn't buy herself new winter coats or boots, but she always scraped together enough money to reconnect our phone and pay the internet bill.

While sorting through my mother's archive after she died, I found nearly two dozen binders of her drawings and notes, some written in blocky capital letters resembling a young child's. The drawings were hard to look at. Many depicted small children bound in devices meant to restrict their movements or physically harm them. My insides flooded with static if I looked at them for too long.

As my mother was dying, I was haunted by the knowledge that her archive would become my responsibility after she was gone. Now, I am haunted by my decision to destroy it. I never doubted the truth of her story, but I have spent most of my life afraid to look at it head-on. After a decade of grieving, I am piecing her story back together in fragments.

My greatest regret is obliterating most of the evidence she left behind.

My mother has been in the hospital for four days. She arrived by ambulance. Calling the paramedics felt like a betrayal, but I was alone. I didn't know what else to do when I found her on her bedroom carpet, where she had been lying for hours after falling in the night on her way to the commode. I appraised her desire to die at home against my inability to lift her limp body, batting the words *dead weight* out of my mind as I dialled 9-1-1.

The red woollen blanket she asked me to bring from home is spread across my mother's legs, its bright colour a contrast to the bland blue-grey of the hospital room. She wears soft white-flannel pyjamas patterned with flowers. On the first day, she was agitated, intent on escape, certain the nurses were out to get her. I had to hold her back to stop her from fleeing the hospital bed on legs too weak to hold her. Now, she looks relaxed, kept calm by palliative sedation. The only movement in her slight frame is the rise and fall of her chest.

I watch closely, wondering when it will still.

At thirty-four, I sometimes feel too young to be responsible for a dying parent, but I am the only relative she trusts enough to do it. I have been preparing for years, but I still don't feel ready when a palliative care nurse named Marlene brings me into a small windowless office to tell me my mother might need my permission to die.

I enlist the chaplain, a Catholic priest who knows my mother from community gatherings, to lead me and three of her closest friends in an impromptu ritual. He obliges my request to leave out the God stuff. My mother is deeply spiritual, but she has heard too many accounts of abusive priests to have faith in organized religion.

We share memories of my mother as the sun sets outside the window. The March sky slowly darkens over snowbanks lingering stubbornly in the hospital parking lot.

It has been a long winter.

"She always called me back," my mother's friend Sandra tells us, her voice breaking. "She listened, and she cared." She recounts how my mother supported her and her family after her sons were sexually abused by a teacher.

"You saved your mother from an attachment disorder," Sandra says, gazing softly at me. "Becoming your mother gave her the capacity to love, and she passed on this gift to me."

I feel the truth of Sandra's words settle across my sternum as I watch my mother lying quietly in her hospital bed, long silver hair fanned out on the pillow behind her. She is still breathing, though more slowly now.

She will be gone by morning.

My mother was not defined by her traumas, but they were one of the shapes she built her life around. So was her love for me.

She and my father, who met and fell in love in Halifax in the mid-1970s, planned to raise me together. Their plans unravelled as my arrival drew near. My father punched my mother in the abdomen when she was seven months pregnant. She fled to Ontario a month later when he abandoned her for a new girlfriend. "You were conceived in love, Zena," she wrote in a pocket-sized spiral-bound notebook when I was two months old. "Then some adult craziness and fear and reality brought you here to be with just me. Ha. Just me. I love your little soul so much. Everything is going to be okay, kiddo."

My mother wanted me to grow up free from violence and was determined to break the cycles of abuse that had reverberated through our family for generations. When I turned one, she wrote these stanzas in a poem called "The 1st Year":

> By day I am the chanter
> of war cries.
> Stay away from my daughter —
> cars in the road
> black dogs
> lightning
> big children who sing
> fee fi fo fum
> I smell the blood of ...
>
> At night, my child —
> twelve months
> three teeth
> fingers agile as a raccoon —
> cries out in her sleep,

mama mama mama.
Then I become the animal
all mothers are —
silent
blood to blood.

One day after swimming lessons, I told her I could see up my instructor's shorts when he squatted at the edge of the pool. We never went back. To my mother, men were more dangerous to me than drowning.

Going through my mother's papers after she died showed me how closely she skirted the edges of despair while I was growing up. She didn't tell me when she was feeling suicidal or in the grip of past traumas, but there is only so much you can hide from a child, especially when it is just the two of you. I was attuned to shifts in our home's atmosphere, like when my mother didn't get dressed in the morning or spoke in unfamiliar voices. I didn't know how many parts lived inside her, but I knew which ones didn't sound or act like my mom.

I am wary of narratives that pathologize survivors or position them as broken, particularly when overlaid with the outsized expectations placed on mothers. What I know is this: My mother loved me with a ferocity bigger than the shadows her traumas cast over our lives. Her devotion to me was like the sun. I knew it was there, even if I couldn't always see it behind the clouds. Its warmth and light helped me grow.

—∞∞—

"Motherhood: made to grow tall and become diaphanous in a way, by the emergence of your child's consciousness. You become tensile, capable of going the limit for their survival. Things sift through you that once would have lodged and hardened."

I found these lines in a small blue, red, and gold journal my mother kept during her pregnancy and my infancy and early toddlerhood. She chronicled her thoughts on motherhood in it alongside accounts of her dreams and the psychic readings she did for family and friends. Years later, she added handwritten yellow sticky-note tabs to the tops of important pages: "Nov. 78 pregnant," "Xena/Zeenah," "Sigman," "Grandma, Kit, Doug and Ron."

Some of these markers are illegible to me now, paths to nowhere. Others lead me here: piecing together a collection of fragments, objects, and memories into the story of my family.

I inherited my mother's journals when she died. The only ones I kept were from when she was pregnant or I was very young. They are an intimate account of early motherhood from before her trauma history became central to our lives and her self-documentation.

When I turn to the page marked "Xena/Zeenah," I find this entry from December 1978: "Xena if it's a girl. ZEENAH. I think it will be a nice name to croon, plus she can be proud of it when she's older." At four months pregnant, my mother was already willing me to grow up proud of who I was, intoning my name like a spell.

My mother was an activist, an artist, and a community builder. As an artist, she worked across mediums—photography, collage, textiles, film, and performance art. Uncovering secrets and confronting violence against women were recurring themes in her work. She co-founded two artist-run centres, one of which is still in operation more than thirty-five years later. I spent my early years in collectively run gallery spaces making art out of scrounged office supplies.

I felt sophisticated compared to my peers, who spent weekends at hockey rinks or eating Sunday dinners with their grandparents. None of the other kids in my class got to watch feminist performance art or listen to poetry while drinking Shirley Temples in bars.

I wasn't afraid to be different, but I sometimes longed for the stability of my classmates' suburban homes, where country geese with big blue bows marched in orderly rows along the wallpaper, and all the dishes matched.

I could be the smartest kid in class, but I couldn't hide that my family was poor and I didn't have a dad. I didn't want anyone to know that my mother sometimes struggled with her mental health or why we rarely saw our relatives. I was ashamed of our ever-changing address, our never-full-enough fridge, how our bathtub doubled as my mother's washing machine, how we rode the bus or walked in a northern city where it seemed like everyone else drove a car.

I curated the details about my life that I shared with my teachers or friends at school, omitting any that might draw attention to the differences that felt shameful or risky to reveal. No one had to tell me *It's bad to have a crazy mother* for me to internalize it. I focused on being the best, excelling in art, drama, and public speaking and winning over my teachers. The only B's I would tolerate on my report card were in gym class.

I worked hard to protect my mother and myself from anyone who might threaten to separate us. We relied on welfare and lived in rented apartments, becoming inured to the scrutiny of social workers and landlords. I don't remember her ever saying it out loud, but there was also the ambient threat of her losing custody to my father or my grandparents.

I wanted others to see me as my mother did: smart, creative, beloved, cherished. I thought that if I was good enough, people would know she was a good mother too.

I wanted to protect my family, so I showed only the parts that felt safe to reveal.

It takes courage to tell the truth when you know you will probably get labelled a liar, crazy, or both. The call to believe survivors is louder in the wake of the #MeToo movement. Still, there is a vast gulf between saying those words and trusting in the veracity of people's stories. There is also a hierarchy of credibility in which some survivors are more likely to face disbelief, stigmatization, or punishment because of who they are and what happened to them.

My mother was one such survivor, her history of violence too easily dismissed as a fabrication. In response, she created spaces where she and other survivors were respected as trustworthy narrators of their lives.

In 1993, my mother founded a group for ritual abuse survivors called the Stone Angels, publishing their drawings and stories in a series of eponymously titled journals. She later formed a second group called ACHES-MC (Advocacy Committee for Human Experimentation Survivors—Mind Control). Both were hubs of community organizing, information sharing, peer support, and education for survivors isolated by the nature and impacts of their traumas.

Between 1994 and 1995, she planned a series of conferences called Making Up for Lost Time that brought survivors of severe childhood sexual and ritual trauma together with therapists and community service providers. Survivors came from across Canada to attend; for some, it was their first time gathering with others who had survived similar forms of abuse. In a 1997 interview about these conferences, my mother said,

> Just to be there as a survivor, and to see forty other women and some of the men who were coming forward at that time was tremendously empowering for survivors. I saw many of them begin to speak for the first time. You take away the element of being "crazy," being isolated ... Many survivors are really creative, and very bright people who are excluded in many ways from

> participating in society at large because they have such a hard time functioning. On that level alone, being able to laugh, and to share, and to speak the same language with other survivors—it's hard to put into words what being able to be understood by other people, other women who have gone through the same thing—how much that means.[1]

She created similar spaces for children, once collaborating with a group of boys who had been sexually abused on an art show called *The Talking Village*. She sewed each one a tent of unbleached cotton, which he made into art. Visitors were invited to fit themselves into the boys' tents, the adults getting down on all fours and folding themselves into shapes small enough to see the world from a child survivor's point of view.

My mother became an organizer, community archivist, and memory worker in the aftermath of the Satanic panic of the 1980s that drew widespread attention to, and ultimately discredited, many accounts of ritual abuse. In the early 1990s, experts also began weaponizing the concept of false memory syndrome against survivors in legal battles with their abusers. Popular accounts of this history don't often acknowledge that the False Memory Syndrome Foundation was founded by Peter and Pamela Freyd after their adult daughter, psychologist Dr. Jennifer Freyd, accused her father of sexual abuse.[2]

The dominant narrative of this era is one of malleable minds and moral panics rooted in irrational fears about daycares and Dungeons & Dragons, of false memories planted by inept or unethical therapists. My mother's archive challenged this narrative, documenting the histories that those who systematically silence and discredit survivors would rather see erased.

I may have betrayed her archive, but "believe survivors" is etched into my DNA. How could it not be, when I grew up bearing witness to how trauma affected her life and the lives of her friends and community members? My mother dedicated herself to protecting me from the abuse that would grant me entrance to her fellowship of survivors. That she succeeded is one of her legacies.

Still, part of me is afraid that one day I will wake up remembering, just like my mother did, and everything will change. *Gotcha!* he'll say when I finally meet the bogeyman I have always feared is hiding in the closet of my memories.

I let out an exasperated sigh as I dig deeper into the green garbage bag my mother asked me to search. The wind blows a gust of snow off the roof of the adjoining building. It is four days before Christmas—my mother's last, as it turns out, though I don't know this yet.

"Why can't you just call your nurse practitioner and ask him to order you a new prescription?" I say as I riffle through the trash with gloved hands, feeling for the pills my mother accidentally threw out.

"He told me to stop taking that medication," my mother admits. "But I like it better than the new one he prescribed."

I sit up out of the hunched-over stance I've taken during my search. My mouth gapes as I process the fact that I am elbows-deep in garbage looking for a drug my mother isn't supposed to be taking. She has just been released from the psych ward after taking an intentional overdose of lorazepam, so I am feeling especially sensitive about the importance of following her health-care providers' instructions.

"I'm not finding those pills for you!" I say, cheeks suddenly hot.

My mother snatches the bag from me.

"Fine," she says. "I'll do it myself!"

"At least put on a pair of gloves," I say, rolling my eyes like an exasperated teenager. No matter how much therapy I do, it's hard not to regress into my sulkiest adolescent self around my mother.

Relenting, she puts on the disposable gloves I hand her. She sits on a kitchen chair, methodically transferring the contents of the full trash bag to an empty one.

Her movements grow more urgent as she gets closer to emptying the bag. Her missing pills are nowhere in sight, confirming my suspicion that one of her health-care providers intentionally took them away.

She tries saving a broken cigarette that she finds in the garbage, but I won't let her.

By this point, my mother allows herself only one cigarette a day. She relies on an oxygen tank to help her breathe, dragging the long, clear tubing down the hallway to smoke in her archive. I wonder if she will live long enough to finish the pack of cigarettes on the table.

"The pills aren't in there, Mom," I say, more gently now. I take the garbage bags out of her hands and help her out of her gloves. "Let's get you back to bed."

She leans into me as we slowly walk the short distance to her bedroom, where the effort of climbing into bed saps the last of her energy. I sit facing her, perched at the edge of her mattress, absently stroking the worn fabric of her quilt with my left hand.

"Do you remember how we used to read the book *Love You Forever* when you were little?" she asks.

I nod, instantly recalling the rhyme that repeats throughout the story:

> I'll love you forever,
> I'll like you for always,
> as long as I'm living
> my baby you'll be.[3]

Years later, I'll learn that the book's author, Robert Munsch, wrote these words in tribute to his two stillborn children. He calls it "my song to my dead babies."[4]

In the picture book, a mother rocks her baby son to sleep while singing the rhyme, repeating the gesture as he grows from a boy into a man. Toward the end of the story, when he's an adult, their roles reverse, and the son rocks his aged mother in her bed.

"The other day I wished you would come over and wrap me in a blanket," my mother says. "I wanted you to rock me like the son does for his mother in that book."

I want to lean toward her, to grant my dying mother her wish. Instead, I recoil slightly, as if leaning away will lessen the intimacy of our exchange.

"I ... I don't think I can do that for you," I say finally. "But I'll give you a really long hug."

She nods.

I wrap my arms around her, easily encircling her tiny frame with mine. She gets smaller with every visit. We sit like this for several minutes. My mother is calm, but I feel trapped by how much she needs me. I breathe slowly, concentrating on keeping my breath soft and steady. I don't want my body to give me away.

I wish I were the kind of daughter who could pick up her dying mother and rock her, reciting familiar words of love and comfort. Instead, I sit there hugging her, counting the seconds in my head until it seems okay to let go.

My mother died of chronic obstructive pulmonary disease (COPD) caused by decades of smoking and the cumulative effects of poverty and trauma. COPD is a slow killer. She spent years cycling through a series of health crises and hospital stays that brought us to the precipice of her mortality and back again. We talked daily as her condition worsened, but we avoided conversations about death.

Once, when I mustered the courage to broach the topic of what she wanted me to do with her body after she died, she said, "Put me up a tree in the forest."

"I don't think that's legal, Mom," I said.

"Okay," she relented, "then I want you to cremate me and keep my ashes with you."

"Where would I put you?" I said, picturing the compact condo I shared with my spouse. "I don't want to keep an urn in the living room or put you in a closet with the spare towels."

"You can keep me on the balcony with your barbecue!" my mother said, only half joking.

We quickly changed the subject.

I didn't know how to ask her what dying felt like or how she wanted to be remembered.

I didn't know how to ask her to tell me the stories I was too afraid to hear.

I couldn't foresee all of the questions I would have for her after she died, or the grief of knowing she would never be able to answer them.

When I think back on this time, I feel alternately compassionate for my past self and regretful of things I didn't do for my mother. My journal entries from this era are angry and heartbroken. I was in my early thirties, suddenly thrust into the role of caring for a dying parent. We lived several thousand kilometres apart, me in Vancouver and her in Thunder Bay. I read books about death and grief as I flew back and forth across the country, but no one had written a manual for this kind of loss.

I couldn't turn to my relatives for guidance. What I really wanted was for someone older and wiser to tell me what to do. It was the only time I have ever wished to be part of a faith community. I yearned to be swept up by a cadre of competent elders. *You don't have to do this alone*, I imagined them saying. *We will show you what to do, and we will make it sacred.*

I wanted to feel like someone's precious child, not the adult in charge.

But I was the adult in charge. It was the hardest thing I have ever done.

I trust that I did the best I could. I know I made mistakes.

My regrets sometimes feel like a bruise I can't stop poking. They are a tender purple wound beneath the surface of my skin that I touch over and over, delaying healing.

My mother's apartment had seven rooms branching off a central corridor. I walked through her home every visit, mentally cataloguing its contents. *Someday I'm going to have to deal with all of this*, I would think. She wasn't dead yet and my inheritance already felt like a burden.

The kitchen, a bright, sunny space that doubled as her office, was my favourite room. Her houseplants thrived there, and the coffee maker was always on. Her fridge was a colourful assemblage of photos of me, her friends, and their kids and grandkids, interspersed with postcards and images she had cut out of magazines. When she was well enough, she could usually be found in the kitchen with the radio on, CBC Radio 2 playing in the background as she drank coffee, smoked cigarettes, and caught up on the day's news.

Her utility room was just down the hall from the kitchen. It was where she did laundry on an old wringer washer, hanging her clothes to dry on a tall wooden rack. This was also where she kept a collection of chronologically organized plastic totes filled with art, toys, clothes, and other mementoes from my childhood. She had archived me too.

Gravity worked differently the closer I got to her archive, an invisible force dragging me into the ground as I approached the big street-facing room at the end of the hallway. My mother kept the accounts of her abuse there alongside documentation of other survivors' experiences, historical research, court documents, case files, newspaper articles, reports, zines, and artwork. Its walls were lined with tall wooden shelves and four-drawer filing cabinets full of papers, books, photographs, audio and video recordings, and other miscellaneous objects.

Everything was meticulously organized: folders in alphabetical order, binders with handwritten labels on their spines, newspaper clippings filed by topic and date of publication. I even found a package of labels labelled "Labels."

Her apartment sat at the corner of a busy intersection with a view of a gravel parking lot and a small urban park. When she became too sick to leave her home, she started smoking in her archive, where she could watch the world outside through a pair of tall windows streaked with dirt and exhaust fumes.

After she died, I found several pages of lined paper near the ashtray where she had kept a running tally of what she saw:

one person walking
one person walking
one person walking
nesting birds flying
one child walking
two people walking
one person walking
one man walking
one woman walking
two people walking
one person walking
red coat walking

It was the loneliest thing I had ever seen.

Early May sunshine filters through grimy third-floor windows as we empty the room that contains my mother's archive. She has been dead for two months. I have returned to Thunder Bay to pack up her apartment with my spouse and a close friend named Edward, who flew north from his home in Ottawa to help me deal with my mother's stuff. We have five days to complete the job. My aunts, uncles, and cousin won't arrive until the end of the week, just in time for her memorial service. Without my queer chosen family, I would be doing this impossible task alone.

"Honey, why would your mother have a throwing knife in a bag with a bunch of sage?" asks my spouse, their black T-shirt damp with sweat and streaked grey with dust.

I don't know how my mother came to own this particular knife, long and silver with a menacing seven-inch blade, but where and how it is stored gives me an uneasy feeling.

"No idea," I say, my words punctuated by the noise of the packing tape dispenser I'm using to seal boxes. I'm covered in dust too. "But if it's in a bag full of sage, that knife has got to be evil somehow. Put it in the garbage."

Tossing a possibly evil, maybe cursed knife in the trash is probably a lousy way to do an exorcism, but I am in triage mode. My arms and legs are stippled with bruises from carrying heavy boxes and furniture down three flights of stairs. I am trying to give away or donate as much as possible. Anything I can't fit into a compact rented storage locker is destined for the dump.

My mother's friend, a women's studies professor who is familiar with her archive, stops by on the first day to orient us to its contents, which she looked through at my mother's request before she died. The professor advises me on what to keep, what to shred, and what might be too upsetting to look at.

It is she who tells me about what she calls my mother's "stalking binders." Before she became too sick to leave the house, my mother had apparently been following around certain local men and photographing their movements. She didn't trust the cops to protect survivors. She was prey turned hunter, relentlessly searching for the truth.

That night, I write in my journal, "It all feels so normal and so crazy all at once."

By the end of the week, we carry more than two hundred boxes of paper and twenty boxes of books out of my mother's archive. We discard most of the boxes at the city dump, a flat expanse at the edge of town where gulls pick through what humans have left behind. We bring anything that seems too private or graphic for a stranger to stumble upon to an industrial paper shredding company that charges by the box. I pay a man $158.20 to destroy in minutes something my mother devoted years to compiling.

I keep only a fraction of her belongings. It will be two years before I feel able to return to Thunder Bay to repeat the process, distilling my inheritance down to two boxes small enough to carry home with me on the plane.

My mother created her archive independently and lived alongside it. She didn't have the support of a non-profit organization or a university. It arose from her experiences and relationships. In a report on ethical engagement with community archives, the Reciprocity in Researching Records Collaborative writes, "Those who have been disempowered by oppressive systems, those who have been 'symbolically annihilated' ... feel the need to create their own autonomous community archives."[5]

These precious community resources are often difficult to preserve. Archival materials must be processed and stored in ways that enable them to remain accessible and intact. This takes time, money, expertise, specialized materials, and space. Dying in poverty, as my mother did, makes it more challenging to conserve the physical evidence of someone's life. When she died, I inherited her archive along with everything else she owned. I spent the few thousand dollars she had saved up on her funeral expenses and paying an estate lawyer to help fend off creditors. My mother owed nearly $12,000 in unpaid rent and utility bills, so there was no money left to pay for the shipping or storage of her archive.

A librarian I knew helped make it possible for me to donate a small portion of my mother's archive to the University of Manitoba. I discarded the rest, too overwhelmed by grief and the pressures of being my mother's executor to figure out what to do with so many boxes of material. I wish I had felt able to move more slowly and deliberately through the process of sorting through my mother's belongings. Pressed for time and worried about money, I rushed through the task I had dreaded for years in a frantic effort to get it over with.

In the weeks and months after her death, I dodged messages and phone calls from my mother's survivor friends who wanted to know what happened to her archive. They were rightly afraid it would be lost. I felt a hot mix of anger and shame every time one of them contacted me. *You don't understand*, I would think, eyeing the stack of death certificates and unpaid bills on the table beside me.

What I really meant was, *My mother died and I feel broken. Please leave me alone to grieve.*

What I really meant was, *I never wanted this inheritance.*

What I really meant was, *Help*.

I am in my mid-forties now. My mother died at sixty-six. Each birthday brings me closer to outliving her. Several years ago, I trained as a death doula, then became a hospice volunteer. When someone close to me is grieving a loss or preparing for one, I am often one of the first people they call. I have gone from being a younger woman searching for answers in books on grief and death to someone who writes them. I am becoming the person I needed when my mother was dying.

The longer I do this, the more I understand how much I didn't know back then. I try not to get stuck in my regrets. Still, I sometimes wish I could go back in time for a do-over.

The me of today would have picked up her dying mother and rocked her like a baby.

She would have washed her mother's dead body, braided her hair, and dressed her in soft, clean flannel pyjamas.

She would have put her mother's archive in storage and left it there until she was ready to decide what to do with it.

She would have given herself the time and space she needed to be a grieving daughter.

She would have asked for more help.

But I wasn't her ten years ago, and who I am today wouldn't exist without what I went through when my mother died or the decade of grieving that followed. Like birth or death, grief is a portal. It never stops reminding me that the only way through is through.

I have always imagined my mother's version of heaven as her sitting aloft on a fluffy cloud, up high enough to watch my life unfold while keeping her gaze partly trained on others. Death has made her so powerful that she can smite pedophiles with lightning bolts while simultaneously beaming a constant stream of love and protection toward me. Every morning, I pray to my mother, loving ancestor, avenging angel: *Please keep my children safe from harm.*

My mother died before she could meet her grandchildren, an ache I have learned to live with. My daughter is seven. She was born exactly four years and four days after my mother died. Her siblings, three-year-old twins, were born on the same day as my mother. The hospital initially scheduled their delivery for the day before. *So close!* I thought when I heard the date, an ancestral near miss. I laughed when the hospital called to tell us they had moved the twins' delivery to my mother's birthday. "Hi, mom," I said. "Message received."

When I was a newborn, my mother wrote this in the same spiral-bound notebook where she'd explained why she was raising me on her own:

> If you have a child, and I hope you do, you'll understand how I feel about you. There is so much work and care and adjustment and fatigue involved, but just like the books say, I wouldn't trade what you've brought to my life and this new way of seeing things for anything I've ever experienced before.

In an undated letter to my father, also composed when I was a baby, she wrote, "I take good care of her—it's almost like being the guardian of something precious—one certainly doesn't own a child. I feel honoured to tend to her needs."

May my children always know how precious they are to me. May they feel cherished. May they know how honoured I am to care for them. May they carry this knowledge in their bones, just like I do.

Stray balloons—red, yellow, green, blue—drift across the floor. The letters on the homemade orange-felt "Happy Birthday" banner are a little rumpled from being stored in a box for most of the year, but it looks festive hanging above the kitchen table. My partner, co-parents, three children, and I were all born between March and June, so spring is birthday season in our house. In our backyard, small green shoots reach toward the sun. Like my children, they seem to grow a little bigger every day.

"Momo grew in Nana's belly and you grew in Grandma Lynne's belly, right?" my daughter Sasha says. It is my partner Riley's birthday, so we are talking about who made us.

A small, bright flame inside me glows to hear her speak so casually about the grandmother she never met, whose death catalyzed a series of losses that transformed me into a parent. I take care to tell my children about my mother because I want to keep her memory alive for them. They couldn't know her in life, so they will know her as an ancestor. It is not everything, but it is enough.

It is not enough, but it is everything.

THIRTY-NINE STAGES OF GRIEF

1. How I Would Have Defined Grief in 2009

A downward-sloping curve that goes from "more sad" to "less sad."

2. Emergency Contact

December 2009

I didn't know staff holiday parties could be so excruciating. I like my co-workers, but our Christmas luncheon's forced joviality has morphed into searingly awkward semi-consensual improv games. I try and fail to blend into the hotel ballroom's garish red-and-purple carpet. When the emcee announces my name and invites me to join the fun, I half stand at our team's round banquet table, waving coolly like the queen. "No, thank you," I tell him, and sit down. My job description doesn't include posing for themed tableaux with the accounting department.

It is almost a relief when my phone rings, because I will take any excuse to leave this party. The relief fades as soon as I realize who is calling and why.

I'm my mother's emergency contact. A social worker is phoning to tell me she has been admitted to the Thunder Bay Regional Health Sciences Centre with pneumonia. This has never happened before. It scares me. She has COPD and is a heavy smoker, so lung infections are a serious threat to her health.

I didn't know she was so sick. Several days earlier, we were emailing about what groceries to buy for her upcoming trip to Vancouver to spend Christmas with me. The first version of her shopping list was a spare two lines:

tangerines
applesauce

It got longer when I nudged her to tell me what she really wanted:

tangerines
applesauce
Ensure Plus (with calories)
soup Campbell's Scotch broth, rice with chicken
Astro Balkan-style white yogurt (the basic kind)
homogenized milk
bananas
Ritz crackers

The money I send her every month to supplement her disability cheque is never enough. She is as accustomed to depriving herself as she is to hiding from me how sick she really is.

Words like *lung function*, *smoking cessation*, and *discharge planning* hover in the air above me as the social worker and I finish our call. I shift into crisis management mode like I've had a shot of emotional novocaine.

I make a mental list of things to do:

call mom at hospital
cancel her flight to Vancouver
pay to have her hospital cable TV turned on
email her two closest friends to tell them she's been hospitalized
book a flight to Thunder Bay

Turning points don't always announce themselves in real time. I don't know that this will be the first of many hospitalizations, or that I will eventually start phoning the hospital so often I recognize each switchboard operator by voice.

3. What I Wish the Social Worker Had Told Me in 2009

Your mother is very sick. She's going to die, but not right away. This is the world's longest roller-coaster ride, so strap in.

Practise saying the words *dying* and *dead* out loud. Feel how they land on your tongue. Notice what feels heavier in your mouth.

Ask your mother what she wants. Tell her what you need. She may be dying, but she still wants to mother you. Let her. Try to be as honest as possible while accepting that you will lie to protect each other. Learn to listen for the truth between her words. She needs you more than she is able to admit.

Don't punish her for what she has survived. You will regret it.

You are already grieving. Assemble a support team and a survival kit. Listen to your body. Ask for help. Pay attention to who shows up and makes your life easier and who makes it harder. The results may surprise you.

Don't let anyone tell you how to grieve.

Keep a journal. You might want to write about this someday.

4. Email from My Mom, December 23, 2009

Subject: I am home

Hi Zenie,
I am home now. Kind of scary. Miss you terribly.
Mom
xoxoxoxo

5. AM DOING WELL

On January 12, 2010, my mother sends me an email gleefully announcing the results of her at-home respiratory test: "I DON'T NEED OXYGEN AM DOING WELL." She was so stressed about the test she almost couldn't breathe, she says, and is motivated to quit smoking. By the end of the month, she is hospitalized again.

In February, six days after my mother is discharged from the hospital, her mum—my grandma Isobel—dies. My mother suffers another loss when she is still too sick to travel to rural Southern Ontario for her mum's funeral in May.

I travel so often for work that I have favourite coffee shops in every major Canadian airport, but I don't go to my grandma's funeral either, because I don't want to be trapped in the country with my relatives. Instead, I shove my grief into a box and pretend it isn't there.

No one tells me that working too much is a flight response. I have a full-time job and am finishing my PhD while producing queer cabarets and editing a book in my spare time. I say yes to everything but rest, betting on the fiction that if I keep moving fast enough, my feelings won't catch up.

AM DOING WELL.

I get engaged in August, so now I have a wedding to plan too. When people ask if I'm going to be Ms. or Mrs. after the wedding, I tell them, "Doctor."

My mother is hospitalized again in October. In November, I pretend not to be disappointed when she has to watch my PhD graduation ceremony via a live stream. *It's fine*, I tell myself. *She was there when I graduated with my bachelor's degree and again for my master's. She can miss this one.* It is the first major academic milestone that my mother has not been there to celebrate with me.

She sends me money for a fancy wooden diploma frame and emails as soon as she sees me onstage: "I SAW YOU - SO PROUD - GOT TO CRY IN MY KITCHEN INSTEAD OF IN A BIG CROWD AT UBC !!!!"

AM DOING WELL, I tell myself over and over. *AM DOING WELL.*

6. You Have No Idea How Many People Have Tried to Love You Back to Life

In 2011, my mother starts keeping a daily log on lined loose-leaf paper. It is part diary, part record of what she did and who she spoke to that day.

On January 12, still grieving her mum's death the year prior, she writes that there is something her mum wasn't able to say to her before she died. My mother, who used to do psychic readings for family and friends, channels a love letter from her dead mum:

> I AM NOT DEAD YOU KNOW. I AM STILL WITH ALL OF YOU. IF YOU THINK IT ENDS WHEN YOU DIE, YOU ARE WRONG. YOU ARE STILL MY DARLING DAUGHTER. A MOTHER DOESN'T TAKE OFF INTO THE ETHER. PLEASE TAKE CARE OF YOURSELF.

MY MOTHER'S INSTINCTS TELL ME THERE IS MORE GOING ON IN YOUR LIFE THAN YOU CARE TO ADMIT TO ANYONE. I KNOW YOU ARE LONELY AND ISOLATED, LYNNE. TOO MANY THINGS HAVE HAPPENED IN YOUR LIFE THAT I WAS UNABLE TO STOP OR EVEN SEE ... LET YOURSELF BREATHE AND HEAL AND TAKE IN THE CARING THAT IS BEING OFFERED TO YOU. DON'T EVER THINK NOBODY CARES. YOU HAVE NO IDEA HOW MANY PEOPLE HAVE TRIED TO LOVE YOU BACK TO LIFE.

Love,
Your Mum

7. Making Excuses

I visit my mother in Thunder Bay in December 2010, then spend all of 2011 making excuses for why I can't come see her: my job is too demanding; I travel too much for work; my soon-to-be-spouse and I are busy planning our summer wedding and promoting our new anthology.

The truth is, I am mad at my mother for being sick and crazy, so I punish her by not visiting.

I would take it back if I could.

I call or email her almost daily because I am worried about her and feel guilty for living so far away. My relentlessly chipper emails use so many exclamation points they sound fake: "Thanks, Mom!" "I hope you're having a good Monday!" "Hello from Winnipeg!" "Hello from Toronto!" "Hello from New York!" "Exciting!"

My mother's mental health worsens the more isolated she becomes. I temporarily unfriend her when she won't stop commenting on my friends' Facebook posts. We get in a huge fight when she forwards my wedding invitation to our relatives without my permission and I find out because a family member I didn't invite RSVPs.

When I confront her about it in a phone call, she hangs up on me.

In an email the next day, she says, "The worst of all this is how much I hate myself for not being able to come to your wedding." There are no exclamation marks in my reply, which includes the line "Of course I wish you could be at our wedding, but I honestly think it's best for both of us if you stay in Thunder Bay."

I would take it back if I could.

8. Sick, Very Sick

On August 21st, she writes in her daily log, "bad today, sick, very sick." She is hospitalized the next day and not discharged until September 13th. When she gets home, she writes of feeling "trapped" and "watched" by doctors, nurses, and public health. She wants to go outside but is too frail to safely traverse the three flights of stairs from her apartment to the ground floor.

Already tiny, she becomes dangerously thin. In October, she emails my spouse, "(don't tell Zena) I need to get some fattening food in me because I am down to 83 lb and it's scary—."

Her email shocks me into action, but not enough to get on a plane. Instead, I mobilize a few of my friends in Thunder Bay to cook for her and hire short-term private home support until she gets approved for publicly funded services. A rotating cast of home support workers assists her with all the things a daughter is supposed to do: cooking, washing dishes, tidying, and bathing.

My PhD thesis was on the working conditions of home support workers, who are now my mother's primary caregivers. I know everything and nothing about what they do for her.

9. The Honeymoon's Over

In September 2012, a nurse from Thunder Bay phones to tell me that my mother has decided to begin receiving palliative care. There is no cure for COPD, so her health-care providers will shift their focus to managing her symptoms and maintaining her quality of life.

When I hear the word *palliative*, I think, *OH SHIT MY MOM IS GOING TO DIE.*

It's been almost two years since my last visit. I still call or email almost daily, but I haven't stopped making excuses for why I can't come to Thunder Bay. My mother makes a note in her log each time I call, always with a small red heart drawn beside it.

Several days after my conversation with the nurse, my mother phones while I am en route to Los Angeles to visit a lover. I tell her that I am in the airport but not why, because now is not the time to explain polyamory to my mom.

I recall almost nothing about our conversation except the overwhelming surge of panic that I stuff into a suitcase because thinking about my dying mother kills my boner. I treat myself to an overpriced airport manicure—red nails short enough to fuck with. I would rather be my lover's Daddy than be a frightened daughter.

I fly to Thunder Bay two weeks later. My mother's apartment has three bedrooms but only one bed, so I book a room at a bed and breakfast on the other side of town. It is the first time I haven't stayed with her. I feel like I am letting her down by not being with her twenty-four hours a day, but having a place of my own helps me not regress into a petulant teenager when I am with my mother.

The B & B's owner upgrades me to the honeymoon suite when she finds out I am visiting my dying mother. I have a big red jacuzzi tub, a *Saxophone for Lovers* CD, three copies of *Men Are from Mars, Women Are from Venus*, and no fucking idea what I am doing.

10. Books I Read in September 2012

Final Gifts: Understanding the Special Awareness, Needs and Communications of the Dying
Dying Well: The Prospect for Growth at the End of Life

11. Books I Wish I Could Have Read in September 2012

What to Expect When You're Expecting to Inherit Your Mother's Trauma Archive
How to Talk to Your Dying Mom About Death and All the Questions You Should Definitely Ask Before She's Gone
Grief Isn't Only for Dead People: Grieving Someone Who Is Still Here
You Can't To-Do-List Your Way Through Grief but It's Okay to Try

12. Protecting Me from the Truth

I travel to Thunder Bay every few months between September 2012 and March 2014. When I'm not there, I call my mother to check in. Most of the time, we talk around her declining health. On her worst days, when I ask how she is doing, she says, "So-so," then changes the subject. She never tells me when she thinks she is dying or when she wishes she would.

"Is today the day I die?" she writes in her log on April 26, 2013. "I am so scared. Zena is back in Vancouver. I couldn't tell her how bad I feel." A month later, in May, she writes, "Zena, are you okay? I am so sorry it came faster than I thought. I thought I could get better." She adds a note in the margin explaining where to find her power of attorney forms.

My mother feared death and sometimes yearned for it. On November 22, 2013, she writes, "BREATHING SO BAD. SUICIDE TODAY?"

A week and a half later, on December 2, she writes, "I want to be wrapped up and held in a rocking chair like a baby and let go. I am so sorry, so very sorry."

On December 14, she writes, "Each morning is closer to the end ... Zena said she was glad to hear my voice. I felt the same way about calling Mum. I just wanted to hear her voice—missed that terribly. I just don't see a way to get better here, now." I won't read this until ten years after her death, but December 14, 2013, is seared into my memory as the day my dying mother was admitted to the psych ward after taking an intentional overdose of benzodiazepines.

When I call the ward, the nurse who answers asks if my mother can move in with me, seemingly without considering that she is too frail to walk more than a few feet and I live in a one-bedroom condo three thousand kilometres away. "No, absolutely not," I reply.

My mother cries on the phone, desperate to return to the safety of her apartment. "All this for one milligram of lorazepam," she says. I tell her I heard she took fifteen to twenty pills. "It was only eight or twelve," she says. I am angry at my mother and angry for her, shocked by the violence of a health-care system that will institutionalize a dying person for wanting to die.

Later that afternoon, I take my troubles to the mall, where I buy a black, beaded party dress to wear for an upcoming New Year's Eve event I am hosting. "Right now it's easier to be productive than present," I tell a friend who asks how I am coping. The idea that I should let myself feel all the time offends me.

13. Bracing

I keep bracing for my mother's death. It is as if there is a clock above our heads, counting down to an unknown end point. I ask myself over and over, *Is this the year/month/week/day my mother is going to die?*

The answer is no until it is yes.

14. What Do You Do with a Dead Body?

My mother dies at the Thunder Bay Regional Health Sciences Centre at 8:20 a.m. on Friday, March 14, 2014. I am not with her. I was at her bedside for most of the previous day and went home to sleep, so I receive news of her death from a nurse by telephone. The din of my friends' busy kitchen—a giggling toddler flinging Cheerios from her high chair, the kettle boiling for tea, breakfast smoothies whirring in a blender—recedes. I am in a tunnel whose only occupants are me and the sympathetic voice in my ear, telling me my mother is dead.

The nurse asks me to come to the hospital. I assume it is because she needs me to sign forms. I have never dealt with a loved one's death before. I suppose it must involve a lot of paperwork. This turns out to be true, but there are no forms for me at the hospital, only my mother's cooling body.

I am shocked when the nurse leaves me alone with my dead mother. I want to bolt, but I worry she will think I'm callous or weak if I do, so I force myself to stay.

My eyes dart around the room: pale spring sunlight filtering in through the window; the tiny pink flowers on my mother's white-flannel pyjamas; a wooden chair upholstered in blue vinyl; her long, silver hair, a little matted in places, its colour dulled by infrequent washing; a bundle of miniature sponges on clear plastic sticks that we used to moisten her mouth; my mother's face, so familiar and yet not because her essence is gone.

What do you do with a body? I don't mean cremation versus burial, I mean what do you do when your mother's dead body is the first you have ever seen and you suddenly find it within arm's reach?

Do you sing to it? Touch it? Kiss it? Pray over it? Wash it? Wail in sorrow?

I place my palm over her heart. Her chest is still, her weary lungs finally at rest. I will myself to keep breathing as I offer an improvised blessing—*Thank you, I love you, may you be at peace. You were a good mother*, I tell her, stroking her face. I don't feel her spirit with me, only the vast emptiness she left behind.

This brief moment of reverence is all I can tolerate. I slink out of her room like a weasel, a bag of clothes she'll never wear again gone leaden in my hand.

15. Learning to Grieve

"There's no template for this experience," I write in my journal on March 17, 2014. "Yet I'm searching for ways to avoid the hidden traps, to make my journey through grief easier."

My mother has been dead for three days. I am trying to learn how to grieve.

I google "grieving a loved one after a long illness."

I talk to friends who have had similar experiences.

I ask for advice on Facebook.

I buy books on grief and books by women with dead mothers.

Some of the grief books give me helpful insights into what I am experiencing. Most of the memoirs by women whose mothers died make me resentful. "I want my mommy," I sneer at their affluent suburban stories. I want my mommy too, but I haven't had her for a long time.

It is a relief when I find Ariel Gore's memoir, *The End of Eve*, several weeks later. I buy a copy on my mother's birthday, devouring it in less than a day. Like me, Ariel is a queer femme who cared for her crazy, dying mom. "I feel so relieved to read a dying mom memoir that captures the complexity, the ambivalence, the anger and resentment," I write in my journal. "The coping in the face of sheer fucking craziness."

I have been reading books about grief and death for two years. All I want now are stories that make me feel less alone.

16. 'Til Death Do Us Part

My spouse holds a green duffle bag in the air like a warning. It is our second fight today, the second time they have threatened to pack a bag and check into a hotel for a few nights.

I am so accustomed to our conflicts that this seems normal. We clash, then come back together, hearts scarred, chasing the rush of reconciliation.

My mother has been dead for four days. When I close my eyes, I see her body. I can't sleep through the night. My throat hurts. My heart is tight, like I'm keeping it behind walls. The walls won't hold; my feelings keep leaking through the cracks. My spouse doesn't seem to recognize this version of me, the wife who has lost her ability to pacify.

Why do I feel like I am being punished for coming undone?

Sometimes, the fabric of your relationship rips so badly it can't be repaired. I am too preoccupied with holding the pieces together to grasp the severity of the tear.

17. Am I Bad at Grief or Good at Coping?

I go back to work after using my allotted three days of bereavement leave because I refuse to take vacation time to grieve. If there's anything this experience has taught me, it's that grieving is not a vacation. I might as well get paid.

I wear colourful tops to the office and never leave the house without lipstick on: camouflage. Returning to some semblance of a routine is a relief, though later I will discover the mistakes I made in those raw early days of grieving: a wrong date here, a missed attachment there. Nothing major, but enough to confirm that my usually detail-oriented mind was elsewhere.

Elsewhere: a hospital room. My mother's apartment. On the couch watching *Call the Midwife* because I can only stomach shows that end in birth, not death. Staring at the spreadsheet I made to keep track of everything I am responsible for as my mother's executor.

I am stunned by how bureaucratic death is and how expensive it is to die in poverty. I hire an estate lawyer because I am ashamed to speak directly to everyone my mother owes money to: her landlord, the gas company, hydro, cable. I receive a bill for $17.50 from the hospital where she died. It comes marked with a hot-pink sticker that reads, "All past-due accounts will be placed in the hands of a COLLECTION AGENCY. Please remit payment within 5 days to avoid such action."

I get angry when people treat me like I'm broken or tell me to slow down. One day, my spouse calls me at the office.

"You don't need to do all this today," they say.

Easy for you to say, I think but don't say out loud.

"Take a deep breath with me," my spouse says.

I pretend to breathe along with them while giving my phone the finger.

18. Don't Tell Me How to Grieve

Journal entry, March 27, 2014:

> Don't sound so surprised when you see me and say,
> "You left the house!"
> Don't tell me grieving lasts two years.
> Don't invite me to join a support group for people
> too sad to get out of bed.
> Don't ask me to form a support group for
> motherless daughters.
> Don't assume I took a week off work to grieve.
> Don't give me a long, slow hug and ask,
> "How are *you*?"
> Don't send me a message that includes the phrase
> *gentle hugs*.

19. Brazen

I go to a friend's book launch, my first public event since my mother's death. I dress all in black, then change into a red-velvet blazer before leaving my apartment. "Brazen," I write that night in my journal. "I won't wear widow's weeds. I will find my own way through this."

20. Grief Ritual: Femmes

Five friends and I have planned a long weekend away at a rented house in a forest overlooking the Pacific Ocean. My mother has been dead for a month. I go anyway, because I wouldn't miss it, and because these femmes keep showing that they can hold all of me in my grief.

We hire a friend who is a somatic sex educator to guide us through an ecstatic retreat. It is a way of deepening into a process we began seven months earlier, when we formed a book club around Barbara Carrellas's book *Ecstasy Is Necessary*. We renamed ourselves the Ladies of Ecstasy when we decided we were more femme sex coven than book club.

We begin our retreat by gathering in a circle, where we thank our ancestors in an opening prayer. My thoughts turn to how trauma seemed to untether my mother from her body. Perhaps the spell I am casting will be powerful enough to reach her too.

We spend the days doing rituals, erotically exploring our own and each other's bodies, laughing, crying, eating, and walking in the forest. Our group magic is palpable: I sleep beside a friend and dream about her partner. When another friend orgasms while two people are touching her, the half-burned logs in the living room fireplace ignite into flames.

On the final night of our retreat, I keep feeling as if someone is missing even though we are all seated together around the dinner table. It's unsettling enough that I finally say something. Two others exclaim they've been feeling it too. We sense a presence across the kitchen. It doesn't feel malevolent, just very much there.

Later, I confess to worrying that it's my mother's spirit. Has she been here the whole time, watching me be a naked sex witch? How do you set boundaries with a ghost?

21. Please Don't Be Mad at Me

I pray to my mother's spirit on my lunch break.

Please don't be mad at me, I plead. I am afraid she is disappointed in me for not doing enough, for not being a good enough daughter.

22. Mother's Day

In May, my spouse and I go to Thunder Bay. We arrive on a Monday, finish packing up my mother's apartment with my friend Edward on Friday, hold her memorial on Saturday, and fly home on Sunday.

I didn't mean to book our return flight for Mother's Day. I want to be hypnotized by the familiar routines of air travel: check-in, security, get a coffee, buy a bag of chips and a celebrity gossip magazine, sit and wait for something to happen. Instead, the airport is an assault of maternal sentimentality. Mother's Day stories play on the TVs. There are treacly cards and cheap bouquets for sale in the gift shop. I see mothers and daughters everywhere. I'm not sure what makes me sadder, the little girls in their mothers' arms or the adult women laughing conspiratorially with their moms as they set off on a trip together. Staring at my phone is no escape. I don't want to see anyone's earnest social media tribute to their living mom.

I bring back three things from my trip: a suitcase full of dirty jeans, dusty T-shirts, and the black-wool dress I wore to the funeral; a braid of sweetgrass gifted to me by a survivor who was friends with my mother; and the key to a storage locker where I put her most personal papers. I'm not ready to discard everything she left behind, but I'm not ready to look at it, either.

"I can't believe something I worried about for so many years is over," I write in my journal when I get home, relieved to have finally tackled the dreaded job of packing up her apartment. "Part of me wants to launch headlong into normal life, into 'After.'"

23. After What?

I am learning that my marriage cannot bear the weight of my mourning, which means it cannot bear the weight of me. Staying feels painful but I am afraid to let it go. I have already lost too much this year.

I start sleeping with a stuffed animal because I need something to hold on to.

24. Please Don't Leave

The summer was bad. The fall is worse. In September 2014 I rent an Airbnb for five days to give me and my spouse some space. It is a relief to have a place of my own. There isn't enough room at home for my grief.

I lie alone in a stranger's borrowed bed and say, "Please don't leave me. You're my family." I don't know if I'm talking to my spouse or my mother. Probably both.

25. Stitching Myself Back Together

I spend Thanksgiving weekend in Toronto at the annual queer kink conference I've attended on and off since 2008. My spouse and I go together, but we only play with other people. The fact that I am more comfortable entrusting my grieving body to friends, lovers, and play partners should tell me everything I need to know about my marriage.

One night in the dungeon, a curly-haired queer witch with twinkling eyes and steady hands pierces a row of needles along my sternum. Bright-red blood trickles down my chest, calling me back to my aliveness. Every needle helps stitch me back together.

26. Crucible

On October 29, 2014, I leave the apartment I share with my spouse and close the door on our marriage. I go to work, where I cry so much that the tiny garbage can beside my desk overflows with used tissues.

"Maybe 2014 is a giant crucible of transformation, healing, and letting go," I write in my journal the next day. I listen to the same song on repeat, the one that says we sometimes have to set ourselves on fire when there is nothing left to burn.

I feel shattered, but people keep telling me I am glowing.

27. Power-Bottoming to the Universe

Being a queer pervert has taught me a lot about submission. Grief has taught me more.

I walk through rainy autumn streets to a friend's house, where I am staying until I can rent an apartment of my own. In the distance, car tires swish on wet roads. I stop to look up at the night sky. It's cloudy, but I can glimpse the moon through the trees.

"I don't know why all of this is happening to me," I tell the universe. "But I'm going to stop fighting it."

A tight gripping inside me loosens. It doesn't make the pain go away, but grieving feels a little easier when I surrender to its power.

28. What Stage of Grief Is the Magic Vagina Workshop?

In November, two femme friends and I register for Portal into the Feminine, a weekend-long women's sexuality workshop in Seattle. The facilitator instructs us to bring hand mirrors, which immediately makes me wary. Is she going to tell me my vagina is a portal? Will there be speculums too? I don't want to drive to America just to look at my cervix.

Most of the other workshop participants are straight women with shitty husbands. My friends and I—a trio of polyamorous queer perverts—feel out of place, but we paid a non-refundable registration fee, so we decide to stick it out. On the second day, I refuse the facilitator's invitation to dance erotically with a woman I've never met without discussing our boundaries or consent first. Grief has left me porous. I am protective of what holds me together and who I let in.

On the third day, the facilitator tells us to masturbate while contemplating what we most desire. One of my desires is to grieve for everything I lost this year. Another is to tell my story in a book. I also want to have a lot of kinky sex.

Our hands are slick with our own wetness when we finish the exercise. The workshop leader invites us to serve ourselves lunch at the buffet table. She does not tell us to wash our hands. My friends and I make a beeline for the bathroom, trying to set a positive example by not getting pussy juice in the bean salad.

29. You Knew Before I Did

On December 14, 2014, I am meditating in the living room of my Craigslist sublet when I suddenly find myself face down and crying into the carpet. I don't know why I'm crying so hard. I do it anyway.

Hours later, I recall that today is the nine-month anniversary of my mother's death and the one-year anniversary of her suicide attempt. My body's ability to mark time amazes me. "You knew before I did," I say to my body, a marvel of remembering.

30. I'm Tired of Being Sad All the Time

I spend many winter evenings curled up on the couch under a blanket, where I binge-watch ten seasons of *Grey's Anatomy*. Its cast faces so many calamities I take comfort in knowing their lives are worse than mine.

"I'm tired of being sad all the time," I write in my journal. "All I want to do is lie around watching TV. Just now I had the realization, 'Oh, maybe I'm a little bit depressed.'"

31. Predicting the Future

I am in the grey box of a borrowed university office, stealing an hour from my day job for a phone call with a psychic on the other side of the country. It is January 2015—a new year. I want her to tell me something good is going to happen.

The psychic talks briskly, like she's getting a rapid download from the universe. My right ear is hot. I have a crick in my neck from cradling the phone with my shoulder, but I don't dare shift positions in case I miss something important. The pile of yellow sticky notes beside me on the desk grows as I try to scribble it all down.

"There was recently an unravelling in your life," she tells me, "a brutal sweeping away." She says I will come out of it completely changed, but it will take time for the dust to settle. It's oddly comforting that even a stranger six thousand kilometres away can sense my grief.

The psychic tells me I should write a book about growing up with my mom.

"When you were little, you were really old," she says. "You get younger as you get older." She tells me I am learning to nurture myself.

The last thing she says before we hang up is, "You would make a wonderful mother."

I am single and childless. I sometimes long for a partner, but never for kids.

Oh well, I think. *She can't get everything right.*

32. A Punch in the Chest

I am riding the bus one day in March when I see an older woman with a red walker who reminds me of my mother.

Grief hits me like a punch in the chest. I get off two stops early so I can cry without anyone watching me.

33. First Anniversary

March 14, 2015, is the first anniversary of my mother's death.

"I think my mom would have been proud of the choices I've made this year," I write in my journal. "She would be proud of me for leaving my marriage, and she would be proud of all the ways I've taken care of myself in the face of so much loss, upheaval, and uncertainty." The night of her death anniversary, I dream of my ex-spouse and wake up feeling angry and abandoned.

I go to therapy, where I sit across from my therapist on a blue loveseat with an oversized brown teddy bear beside me. He's been my companion on her couch for almost a year now. I feel too self-conscious to cuddle him but I like knowing he's there. My therapist is the type of older woman who reminds me of who my mother could have been without all the poverty and trauma. I try not to resent her for this. It's not her fault for suffering less than my mother did.

"I'm afraid all of my demons of fear and insecurity will come home to roost," I tell her. She invites me to drop into my body and envision what security would feel like. I imagine myself as a tree surrounded by other trees. Rich soil, water, and air nourish us. Sunlight filters through the canopy, making patterns on the ground. There is a robin's nest in my branches, three blue-green eggs nestled inside.

34. I'm Not Horny, but I'm Not *Not* Horny

The only erotic encounters I've had since leaving my marriage have been with myself or with trusted friends in workshop settings.

I satisfy my need for touch with massages from a queer RMT whose treatment room is a safe place to ask for what I need and practise receiving it. Sometimes, what I need is to cry so hard I drip snot on the floor through the cutout in her massage table. She is always very nice about it.

Summer is coming. Everything around me is in bloom. I am shedding a protective shell after months in a grief cocoon.

A friend from Toronto tells me they are going to a weekend-long queer kink conference in Palm Springs in June. They have room for one more person in their rented house. It seems fated, so I spontaneously buy a ticket.

What do you wear to a play party in the desert? I wonder.

The answer is a sheer black bodysuit.

35. Grief Ritual: Perverts

A wall of desert heat hits me when I step off the plane in Palm Springs. The mid-century modern house my friends and I are staying in for the weekend has a pool, so I don a 1950s-style cherry-print pink swimsuit as soon as I arrive. A small crew of queer perverts is already splashing around. I slingshot myself into the pool with them.

I haven't kissed anyone since October. Now, I am making out with three people at once, flowing between mouths in aquamarine waters. It feels light, free-spirited, the right way to begin.

The conference runs for three days, with a play party each night.

On the first night, I watch.

On the second night, I am ready to play but not to lose control, so I co-top a friend with another femme. She is tall, like me, and reminds me of Barbarella. We amp each other up, kissing and laughing at our depravity while tormenting our obliging bottom. The scene is fun, though I crave something more satisfying. I want to feel freer. I want to let go. I want to leave some of the leadenness of my winter of grieving behind in the desert.

On the last day of the conference, I gather up my courage to talk to the gorgeous woman sunning herself by the pool. She is a motorcycle-riding Leatherdyke and a notoriously ferocious sadist with long blond hair and even longer legs. Her leonine gaze mesmerized me when we cruised each other the night before. I don't want to miss my chance to play with her.

I'm wearing my lucky black bodysuit and red high-heeled sandals. On my way over to talk to her, I pop a stick of gum in my mouth, suddenly self-conscious about my breath.

I wend my way through throngs of nearly naked queer women and trans folks to reach her. She is laid out in a bikini on a chaise longue, like a goddess.

"How are you feeling?" she asks when I perch at the foot of her chair.

"I feel like I should swallow my gum," I confess. How am I blushing already?

"You should," she says, "because I'm going to kiss you."

She pounces, claiming my mouth. We claw at each other like animals, biting and scratching, her hand gripping my throat, her fingers in my cunt.

She unleashes something wild in me. I roar, giving her everything I've got. We play for ten hours, moving from poolside to her bed to a Saint Andrew's cross to grappling in the dirt, taking occasional breaks to fuck, eat, and drink water. I am in awe of her power, and mine, and the alchemy of our powers colliding. She meets the full force of my desire with her own. With her, I am unafraid of being too much. We are ravenous together, and satiated.

I don't call it a grief ritual, but it is.

I fly home to Canada in the only outfit I packed that covers all of my bruises, sweltering in jeans with a long-sleeved shirt zipped modestly up to my throat. I carry traces of her home with me under my skin, a reminder of all the pleasure and endurance my body is capable of.

36. Grief Ritual: Witches

In August, I join two of the Ladies of Ecstasy at a week-long witchcamp in the forests of British Columbia. As a newbie, I'm given the opportunity to buddy up with a more experienced camper. "I choose Riley!" I call out, like a kid claiming dibs on the biggest slice of cake.

We've known each other casually for years, but I've been paying closer attention to Riley since this winter when I dreamed about making out with them. They know about my dream but not the kissing part. I flirt by offering to share the candy I brought with me to camp. "I'll be your snack proxy," I tell Riley, passing them my stash of chocolate-covered almonds and organic fruit gummies from the bulk section at the fancy grocery store.

Kissing them in real life is even better than it was in my dream.

Every evening, around a hundred campers gather for a group ritual. On the second-last night of camp, Riley and several other witches lead us through a rite of grief and transformation. I walk slow circles around the dim wood-panelled recreation hall, opening myself to feeling. Heavy as a stone, grief drags me to my knees. I crumple to the ground, keening into worn linoleum.

Time acts differently during rituals, so I don't know how long I am there before someone's hands land gently on my back. First one pair, then another, and another. I'm not sure who they belong to. It doesn't matter. What matters is that I am not alone. I feel electrified. Energy surges through my chest and arms. My hands tingle with power.

When I finally look up, six or seven witches are gathered around me in a loose circle. Most of them regard me with equanimity, as if my emotional lightning storm were just another weather system passing through the room. One woman pushes a box of tissues in my direction, an uneasy expression on her face. She is trying to comfort me, but her gesture telegraphs, *YOU ARE TOO MUCH*.

I refuse to shrink my feelings down to the size of a Kleenex box.

She's afraid of me, I realize. *Doesn't she know how powerful grief is? Maybe that's what scares her*. I ignore the tissues. My heart softens toward those who fear grief. I was the same way once. Now I am a conduit. *Let it in*, I tell myself, casting my own spell. *Feel it all. Let yourself be transformed.*

37. Time Travel: The Psychic Was Right

Riley told me they were trying to get pregnant before we kissed for the first time at witchcamp. Remember the nest with three blue-green robin's eggs? Riley and I have three kids now. I'm not their mother, but close enough.

38. Grief Ritual: Ancestors

It's October 2015, a week before Halloween. The days are growing shorter as autumn gives way to the rainy darkness of a Vancouver winter. The high-ceilinged rectangular room where we have gathered for a Samhain ritual is warmed by the heat of two hundred bodies. It's the same community hall where I was married. Tonight, I am here to honour my beloved dead.

The veil is thin this time of year, I am told, our ancestors more readily within reach. *Are you here, Mom?* I sometimes wish she would haunt me, just so I could feel her presence again. Instead she shows up in my dreams.

I cast glances at Riley beside me in the circle, the embers of our witchcamp crush slowly kindling into a steady flame. "I have tender feels for you," I told them during our most recent date. It was code for "I'm falling in love with you," an invocation too powerful to say aloud.

I think back to my first Samhain ritual a year ago, in October 2014. My mother had been dead for seven months. My marriage was on life support. I had never gone to a large public ritual before. I felt awkward, like someone would surely sniff me out as an imposter. I stayed because I needed to hear the priestess say my mother's name like a prayer. When we sang together, hundreds of voices rising into the rafters, I understood why other people went to church.

Last year was my season of loss. Now, I am creating something new in the ashes of everything that burned in its wake.

I join hands with Riley. We dance a spiral, our bodies fractalling into infinity.

39. How I Would Have Defined Grief in 2015

You aren't who you used to be. Ask yourself: Who has grief helped me become?

AFTER WIFE

The End

The second joint of my left ring finger ached and swelled the closer I got to the end of my marriage. It hurt to put on my wedding band, but I wore it anyway.

I would rather endure the pain than answer questions about why my hand was bare.

It wasn't so much that I expected a happy ending. It was that I felt responsible for delivering one. Our love story wasn't supposed to end in failure. The slender white-gold band symbolized our love and commitment. What would it mean to remove it after only three years?

I swallowed the pain for months, pretending the fire inside wasn't a sign of something burning. Fire feeds on oxygen. My finger blazed. I was suffocating.

My spouse and I got married in a rented community hall where our Leatherdyke friends sometimes hosted play parties. It seemed fitting to get gay-married in the room where we once had a threesome with a stranger. We were after something queerer than "love is love." Neither of us thought marriage meant monogamy or a lifetime of vanilla sex, but part of me still believed that the most successful relationships ended in death.

It's why I sometimes fantasized about my spouse dying young of a tragic illness so I could escape our marriage without the stigma of divorce. *'Til death do us part.* In the end, it was death that parted us. My mother died in March. My marriage ended in October. Our wedding vows withstood barely three seasons of grieving. Would I still be married if my mother were alive today? Probably not, but her death fuelled the flames licking at my fingers.

My spouse and I were together for eight years, married for three. The best parts of our love—laughter, passion, creativity, adventure—patched over the cracks in our relationship, but the edges wouldn't hold. An accumulation of small slights and unhealed wounds collected in the spaces between us. I seethed quietly, screaming into towels, and looked for answers in self-help books. I saved my ugliest feelings for my journal, where I could tell the truth without consequences. Unwilling to trust my spouse with the bounty of a full meal, I scattered my vulnerability like crumbs, reserving the sweetest mouthfuls for close friends and lovers.

For years, I coiled myself into an emotional shock absorber, there to buffer my masculine partner against unwelcome feelings. Grief undid me, then moulded me into a new shape. My spouse seemed not to recognize who I became after death eviscerated my capacity to placate. When I wouldn't go back to who I had been before, they questioned my sanity and looked for a replacement.

Several months after my mother died, my spouse told me they wanted to start dating someone new. We were polyamorous, so I tried to be okay with it, but loss had ravaged the landscape of my attachments. I alternated between rage, panic, and stony calm, lashing out at my spouse and their girlfriend. "It's like my inner child is riding around on my inner guard dog while shooting an AK-47," I told my therapist.

I took up running, spent my lunch breaks on the treadmill. I ran in place for hours, trying to escape what my life had become. My spouse and I went to couples counselling and fought on the drive home.

In the end, it was me who left. The swelling on my finger didn't subside until six weeks later. By then, I had a place of my own—a downtown condo rented from a stranger on a three-month backpacking trip with her boyfriend. I built an altar to myself in their bedroom, a blank white square with a view of the city, and covered their queen-sized mattress in soft, pale-green flannel sheets.

I refused to give my spouse my new address. I wanted more than walls between us. I wanted to be unfindable. We would see each other on my terms, or not at all. I held fast to the boundaries of my sanctuary, only permitting across the threshold those who had proven themselves worthy of apprehending the vastness of my mourning.

It was in this temporary refuge I first began exploring who I could become after wife, after marriage, after the future I had imagined was suddenly gone.

The Beginning

I had a crush on my spouse for years before we started dating. I remember the first time I saw them perform at the Sugar Refinery, a now-defunct venue in downtown Vancouver. They shone, captivating me with their charisma, talent, and a kind of queer masculinity that left me humming with longing. I made a point of saying something to them after the show. I don't recall our exchange, only that I wanted them to notice me.

Just barely out of the closet, I was learning to hold the word *femme* in my mouth like a sacrament. As I grew into my queerness, I joined a community of writers and artists who brought me into proximity with my crush. I wasn't a peer, but I wasn't just a fangirl, either.

We bumped into each other at readings or our neighbourhood coffee shop often enough to become friendly acquaintances. I would mentally replay each encounter afterward. Was I imagining the flirtatious vibes between us? Did I seem cool (gay) enough? My crush, ten years older, had been out for much longer than me. I affected an air of mature worldliness as a cover for my insecurities.

Already indie-queer famous when we met, my crush's audience kept growing as they published and performed more widely. I read all of their work and went to their shows, even after I met and fell in love with my first long-term girlfriend. I remember how my heart sank when I read my crush's story about getting engaged to their then partner. "I missed my chance," I sighed. I was single again and fantasizing about being romanced by a handsome butch.

My crush was nursing a recent heartbreak when our orbits finally collided after five years of flirting. They were in an open relationship then too. This time I was the new girl. We fell into bed and didn't surface for days, sustaining ourselves on midnight meals of pork chops and sautéed mushrooms.

We took a spontaneous road trip where one night we fucked so vigorously that things fell off the walls of my crush's trailer. It was on this trip that we had our first big fight. No one I dated had ever yelled at me before. Everything about us was passionate, I reasoned, even our disagreements. The makeup sex was worth it. The next month, I ditched grad school for a week and bought a last-minute ticket to Amsterdam when they went on tour in Europe. We drank coffee on patios, explored the red-light district, and pretzelled ourselves into shapes small enough to have sex in our hotel room's twin beds.

We made our relationship official after their ex-fiancée moved out, spending as much time together as we could around my crush's tour schedule. I made mix CDs of love songs for when we were apart. The heady atmosphere of our new romance was the perfect environment for me to bloom into a more vibrant version of my femme self. I wore clothes that telegraphed my desires: lace lingerie sets, form-fitting pencil skirts, and vintage-style dresses with nipped-in waists. My vision of being the glamorous femme on a dapper butch's arm was finally coming true. I wanted to look the part.

I would be the dream girl, the whole package, worthy of a happily-ever-after: someone kind, smart, and pretty enough to bring home to your mom, filthy enough to act out your wildest sexual fantasies with, and emotionally self-sufficient enough for two people. I would win at love, the femme who caught the eye of the hottest butch in town and held their gaze forever.

If you read between the lines of the history of marriage, you'll find the history of divorce. In her book *Marriage: A History*, historian Stephanie Coontz documents how the symbolic meaning and practical purposes of marriage shifted over time. Prior to the late eighteenth century, marriage functioned more explicitly as an economic and political institution, not a sentimental or romantic one. "For centuries, marriage did much of the work that markets and governments do today," Coontz writes.[1] Marriage became sentimentalized in the nineteenth century. With it came calls to make it easier to end such unions: "No sooner had the ideal of the love match and lifelong intimacy taken hold than people began to demand the right to divorce."[2]

Same-sex marriage was legalized in three provinces (Ontario and British Columbia in 2003 and Quebec in 2004) before it was legalized across Canada in 2005. Michael Leshner and Michael Stark, who initiated the case legalizing gay marriage in Ontario, were Canada's first same-sex couple married in a civil ceremony.[3] Leshner and Stark wed to great fanfare and considerable media coverage on June 10, 2003, just hours after the Ontario Court of Appeals declared its favourable ruling.[4] Hundreds of other couples soon followed suit, including two lesbians known only by the initials M.M. and J.H., who married on June 18, 2003.

Unlike Leshner and Stark, who celebrated their twentieth wedding anniversary in 2023, M.M. and J.H. separated after five days of marriage, ending a ten-year partnership. They filed for divorce in 2004. "I had naively hoped that marriage would help resolve some of the issues in our relationship, but unfortunately it was not a solution," M.M. later said in an affidavit. "I was aware almost immediately after the ceremony that it was a mistake."[5]

Theirs was Canada's first same-sex divorce case, and it confronted a problem: The federal *Divorce Act* defined a spouse as "either of a man or a woman who are married to each other."[6] In an opinion piece, lesbian legal scholar Brenda Cossman pointed to how, at the time, "many dimensions of marriage and divorce law [hadn't] caught up with the new reality of same-sex marriage."[7] She gave the example of how, for centuries, courts had tended to define adultery—one of several grounds for divorce—as heterosexual intercourse. "Equal access to marriage requires equal access to its exit options," Cossman wrote in 2004.[8]

When I first learned about M.M. and J.H.'s case, I wondered if they pursued it as a form of legal activism. Fighting for the right to divorce after the boys got all the gay marriage glory seemed like a dykeishly pragmatic thing to do. But as I pieced together what happened by reading twenty-year-old newspaper articles, I found traces of a more intimate story. In an account of the September 2004 hearing where a judge granted their divorce, the reporter described how M.M. "sat quietly to one side of the courtroom, dressed in grey pants and vest and wearing a grey and pink tie. At times she held the hand of a female companion for support."[9] Her soon-to-be ex-spouse, J.H., wasn't there. The couple pursued their case anonymously to "avoid the embarrassment and the 'stigma' of being the first divorced gay couple" in Canada.[10]

Only M.M. and J.H. know the truth of what happened between them. The fact that they are known by their initials and chose to pursue their case anonymously makes me wonder if the burden of others' judgments was too much to bear. Photos of Leshner and Stark's first kiss as a married couple made it into newspapers around the world. M.M. and J.H.'s story, by contrast, was presented more matter-of-factly as a coda to the main event, a curiosity for newspaper readers to consume with their morning coffee.

In 2023, several media outlets featured stories celebrating Leshner and Stark's twentieth wedding anniversary.[11] None published articles commemorating the twentieth anniversary of M.M. and J.H.'s divorce. I wonder where they are now. Are they happy? Is M.M. still holding the hand of her female companion for support? Did M.M. and J.H. eventually become friends, or have they been awkwardly avoiding each other at lesbian potlucks for two decades? Do they ever think about how their breakup changed history? Leshner and Stark may have won the right to marriage, but M.M. and J.H. were the first to carve an escape route.

Becoming a Main Character

My relationship with my crush began privately when our first kiss sparked a passionate affair, but it became part of a public narrative as we grew into a more established couple. My crush-turned-partner was a writer whose work took inspiration from their life, so our love story eventually made its way into their books and performances. Listening to their stories about our relationship was like hearing the best versions of us rendered for an audience who would laugh, cry, and applaud in all the right places. Our conflicts never made it onto the page.

I became a main character when I went from fan to girlfriend. Audience members would turn to look when my partner pointed me out at shows, delighted by the novelty of seeing someone from a book in real life. Other femmes sometimes glared like they were challenging me to a fight. My partner had a devoted fan base, so I assumed the glarers were jealous that I had captured their literary crush's heart. I would smile graciously, conscious of looking pretty without seeming conceited. Meanwhile, a petty little voice inside me singsonged, *I won*.

My partner and I became a butch-femme couple in the late 2000s and early 2010s, during a time of renewal and resurgence in these identities. There were annual conferences, events, and online and in-person communities, all with the aim of fostering pride and strengthening connections among butches and femmes. Vancouver even had all-femme and all-butch choirs. Queer audiences hungry for representation cherished my partner's books and stories. Videos of their odes to butches and femmes racked up tens of thousands of views. Our love story was proof that butch-femme romance still flourished.

We leaned into our status as a queer power couple, producing events together and co-editing an anthology on butch and femme identities and desires. When our book was published in 2011, we toured several North American cities, reading to sold-out rooms of fabulously dressed queers. We posed for photos on the red carpet in New York when our anthology was nominated for an award.

I liked being in the spotlight. It fed the part of me that had always wanted to be exceptional. Going from fan to girlfriend gave me more control over the narrative, but who I could be was always limited by the role I felt obligated to perform.

When Anjali Chakra and Sufi Malik broke up, it made *The New York Times*.[12]

The couple, who had been dating for six years and engaged for two, had nearly five hundred thousand followers on Instagram and more than 135,000 YouTube subscribers when they called off their engagement just weeks before their wedding.[13]

Chakra, who is Hindu and Indian, and Malik, who is Muslim and Pakistani, were catapulted into internet celebrity when photos celebrating their queer South Asian interfaith relationship went viral in 2019. The pictures garnered more than 130,000 likes and attracted the attention of media outlets in the US, India, Pakistan, and the UK.

"Both of us had our own battles to accept our sexuality," Chakra and Malik said in a 2020 interview, "so having such widespread support was wonderful and validating."[14] The couple became engaged in 2022, sharing a twenty-five-minute long video of their proposal on YouTube. A devoted community followed along with the couple's wedding plans.

Fans were shocked when the couple called off their nuptials in March 2024, after Malik admitted to cheating. "As a South Asian who has never found queer representation and comfort in our community, Sufi and Anjali were the two people who we've closely looked up to and now they've broken up too," one person posted on X.[15] Zuvariya Shaikh, who had been following the couple's relationship since 2020, called their breakup "nothing short of devastating."[16]

In a series of videos chronicling her breakup recovery process, Chakra talks about how the "very stressful, very public" split turned her life upside down.[17] She tells of experiencing overwhelming feelings of sadness, loneliness, and despair, as well as insomnia, hair loss, and sudden and drastic weight loss. Malik kept a lower profile online after the breakup. Some cast her as the villain because of her role in their split. Despite Chakra asking that her ex not be shown any negativity, Malik was targeted with Islamophobic and homophobic slurs. Lesbian writer Kayla Kumari Upadhyaya called the backlash against her "outsized and mean."[18]

Whenever I see queer couples building social media brands around their relationships, I always wonder, *But what will you do when you break up?* My former spouse and I fell in love when Instagram was brand new and TikTok hadn't been invented yet. It's easy to imagine us taking advantage of platforms like these, had they been available to us, and a relief that we couldn't. It was hard enough when a fan of my ex's work messaged me two years after our marriage ended, demanding an explanation for our breakup.

I understand the allure of being #CoupleGoals. Feeling validated in your relationship is a powerful antidote to the messages many of us have internalized that queer love is wrong. Yet my experiences have made me wary of what can happen when we make ourselves into characters in a love story. Even writing this book feels risky. Am I doing it again?

A Swirl Cone of Romance and Pragmatism

I came out as queer shortly before British Columbia legalized same-sex marriage, so I took for granted that I would someday get married. It seemed like the natural next step in our relationship when, after several years of dating, my partner and I got engaged. I was, in sociologist Abigail Ocobock's terms, a "marriage assumer"—a queer person who had always had access to same-sex marriage and saw it as an inevitable end point in their relationship trajectory.[19] I had a vague sense that marriage was bad if it made you a man's property, but naively assumed that queerness would let me bypass the parts of the institution that didn't align with my politics.

My perspective on marriage was a swirl cone of romance and pragmatism, its flavours mingling into something smooth and easy to swallow. Wearing an engagement ring signalled something important about me: I had been chosen. Marriage was proof of my value and desirability, a new level of adulthood unlocked. By becoming a wife, I transcended my girlhood. I didn't want to be a mother, so this was as womanly as I was going to get.

Marriage offered a promise of security, and I wanted a say in who was legally defined as my family. My years as an LGBTQ+ health advocate had taught me to be wary of what can happen when doctors or other authority figures don't believe us when we tell them who our family is. Having been raised in a family riven by abuse and estrangement, I clung to the idea of marriage as a safeguard against abandonment. I knew not all marriages lasted forever, but I hoped my partner and I would beat the odds. For me, happily ever after was a future where I was loved, safe, and not alone.

"Love is an exploding cigar which we willingly smoke," read our wedding invitations, quoting Lynda Barry. Neither of us had grown up with parents in long-lasting happy unions. Getting married was a chance for my partner and me to rewrite our inherited stories about romantic love. Our shared embrace of non-monogamy seemed like insurance against cheating while rejecting the idea that one person was capable of meeting all of our needs.

In her book *Marriage Material: How an Enduring Institution Is Changing Same-Sex Relationships*, Abigail Ocobock points to the "messy mix of resistance and conformism" characterizing same-sex marriage.[20] Her research found that queer people's attempts to do marriage differently butt up against taken-for-granted ideas about what marriage means, ideas that "seep into their beliefs and practices even as they attempt to resist institutionalized ways of doing things."[21] In *Queering Marriage*, sociologist Katrina Kimport describes marriage as an institution with normative power that acts on people in unanticipated ways.[22] Same-sex marriage preserves this institution while expanding its boundaries, conferring feelings of safety, inclusion, and societal validation along with access to a host of legal and financial benefits.

In 2004, the US General Accounting Office reported that marital status is a factor in determining rights, privileges, and benefits under more than 1,100 federal statutory provisions.[23] This figure became an argument both for and against same-sex marriage, including among queer activists on opposing sides of the marriage equality debate. Those in favour of expanding marriage rights positioned access to these benefits in terms of equity and civil rights. Activists critical of marriage called for expanded access to health care, social security, citizenship, and other benefits without coercively tying them to marital status.

As a marriage assumer, I didn't think too hard about marriage as a legal and financial institution. "The thing people don't tell you about marriage is ... it's a contract," says Karl Dunn, a divorced gay man. "You've just signed away the ownership of your relationship ... to the government. They own it now."[24] Buying a marriage licence was easy—I picked ours up for a hundred dollars at a local drugstore chain. It was just another thing on my wedding to-do list. I didn't stop to question what it meant to put our relationship into a form so acceptable to the state that it required a licence.

My spouse-to-be and I quickly got caught up in the pageantry of planning our elaborate celebration. It was all about *getting* married. I don't remember us ever asking ourselves what we would do if we had to get out of it.

East Vancouver's Royal Wedding

I wore hot pink to my wedding because I wanted to be a bride but not look like one.

In a photo from that day, I stand alone in our venue's front hallway wearing a fuchsia-silk dress tailor-made from a 1950s pattern that shows off my décolletage. A slim pink belt with an oval rhinestone buckle sparkles at my waist, the two crinolines under my skirt filling out my retro silhouette. My face is covered by a rhinestone-studded black veil attached to a black beaded fascinator adorned with feathers and bright-pink flowers. Right hand cocked on my hip, I look into the camera with a defiant tilt to my chin.

I have the poise and confidence of a woman standing on a peak, surveying a panorama of possibilities. I don't know that in three years, it will all be over.

We spent months planning our celebration with a crew of friends, approaching it as if we were producing our best-ever (and biggest-budget) queer cabaret. Our guest list grew to nearly 150 people, with friends and family flying in from as far away as Europe to join in the celebrations. It was a very good party, even if the photos are hard for me to look at now.

Our wedding was several months after Kate Middleton's much-hyped marriage to Prince William, so our venue dubbed our nuptials "East Vancouver's Royal Wedding" on its monthly event calendar.

I remember my wedding in flashes, because it went by in a blur: Posing for photos before the ceremony with my spouse-to-be, late afternoon sunshine beaming on our smiling faces. Eight friends doing jazz hands around us as we shared our first kiss as a newly married couple. Turning our first dance to Journey's "Don't Stop Believin'" into a group singalong. Reminding myself to eat the oysters we had splurged on. Crying to the love song a musician friend wrote for us. Taking group photos of the butches and femmes posing like royalty on the stage. Closing the night with steamy burlesque performances for an adoring crowd of queers and visiting uncles.

We shared a few photos of our wedding on the Tumblr account I created for our butch-femme anthology. In one, my grey-suited spouse dips me while sitting on a red throne. In another, we smile for the camera while posing with my spouse's small, fluffy dog. It felt good to share our joy with a wider community, especially since the US still hadn't legalized same-sex marriage.

"I love this!! And I love them!!" read one comment on our post. "They're so cute. I hope I'm lucky enough to have an adorable dykey wedding one day," read another. I was so focused on inviting others to share in our happiness that I didn't think about how it would feel if we broke up. Things between us weren't always easy, but we had promised ourselves and our communities a love story.

What else could we do but deliver one?

As part of US campaigns to legalize same-sex marriage, LGBTQ+ rights organizations held focus groups with politically moderate Americans. They learned these voters didn't view marriage as a legal institution. They saw it as a way of validating relationships, so marriage equality campaigns strategically centred the idea of marriage as a symbol of care, commitment, and love. Marriage was presented as a way to protect children and keep families intact. Couples at the centre of legal battles over marriage equality were chosen for their ability to conform to these narratives.[25]

Julie and Hillary Goodridge, a lesbian couple with a daughter named Annie, were the named plaintiffs in the case that led to the legalization of same-sex marriage in Massachusetts. They later described the experience as traumatic.[26] Under pressure to seem perfect during the three-year legal battle, Hillary said she carried "the stress of feeling like I have the entire community resting on our being likable ... We had to look like the girls who could be next door. Not too threatening."[27] Media outlets clamoured for footage of the women ironing or flipping pancakes.

The Goodridges won their case and were married on May 17, 2004. The protracted legal battle put added strain on their relationship, as did the media attention it attracted. Opponents of same-sex marriage sent out a hateful mass mailing to every family at their daughter's school.

Then–US President George W. Bush referenced their case in his State of the Union address.

Despite their struggles, the women forewent couples counselling. "It felt like too much of a risk," said Julie, who worried word would get out.[28] Instead, they kept their distance from each other at home. The Goodridges separated in 2006, after two years of marriage, and divorced in 2009. When news of their split was leaked to the media, they received a nasty email from another queer person telling them at length about how their divorce was destroying the LGBTQ+ community. Annie, who was ten when her parents separated, described feeling like her family had "let everyone down."[29]

To fail at achieving a love that lasts forever is to disappoint those whose dreams are tethered to our success while giving fodder to those who believe our love could never be real. It is not enough to try; we must defy the odds. Under these terms, anything less than "'til death do us part" is a failure.

Some Promises

The night I realized my marriage was over, I was lying on the brown-leather couch my spouse and I bought when we moved in together. We had chosen it carefully, imagining ourselves curled up there reading books or watching scary movies. Now it was doubling as a makeshift bed. I had volunteered to sleep on the couch after hours of fighting bitterly with my spouse, who was shut away in our bedroom. I slept better alone.

We had just reunited after several weeks apart while my spouse was on tour. I came home from work that evening feeling cautiously optimistic about a planned date night. Instead, we started fighting and didn't stop. We were trapped in an exhausting cycle of clash-retreat-repair, except repair didn't feel possible anymore. I was sick of putting band-aids on fractures and expecting them to heal.

The refrigerator hummed in the background as I flopped around under a blanket, trying to get comfortable. No matter what position I took, nothing felt right. *It's over*, I thought. *I can't stay here anymore*. I didn't mean the couch. A bracing wave of clarity washed over me like cold salt water. Instead of falling asleep, I was waking up to the realization that after months of agonizing over the state of my marriage, I was done.

As a bride, I thought of my wedding vows as a promise to try our hardest to stay together. As a wife, I learned that keeping this promise asked too much of me. I made a new vow to myself that night: I would leave everything behind to find out who I could become on the other side of loss.

When I left our apartment the next morning, my spouse threatened to change the locks. I went to work and didn't come home until two weeks later. My spouse was on tour again, so I had the place to myself. It was the only condition under which I would return.

I pulled eight years of journals out of storage on my first night back, searching for evidence to support my decision to leave. What patterns had I overlooked or chosen to ignore? The result was a tightly spaced four-page chronology showing how we had been locked in the same dance for years.

I told no one but my journal when I fantasized about us breaking up, or about how my spouse threatened to divorce me just shy of our first wedding anniversary. Only my closest friends and the couples counsellor we eventually started seeing knew we were struggling, but I kept the worst of our conflicts to myself. Even as our relationship unravelled, it still felt natural to be the most affectionate and charismatic versions of ourselves in public. Our masks came off in private. My journal entries were a reminder that when we showed each other our true faces, we reacted with fear and contempt. The wounded animals in us, scratching and snarling, desperate to feel seen, clawed at each other or ran away.

We loved one another deeply and were often happy during our eight years together, but our relationship wasn't the safe haven I needed it to be. After our wedding, we talked about getting matching tattoos as a sign of devotion. We never followed through. Something in me was wary of such permanence. A ring I could take off. A tattoo was forever.

Ten years later, I'm grateful to my past self for her reluctance. Some promises aren't meant to be etched into my skin.

The Truth Is More Complicated and Not as Pretty

Although we had been together for five years when we wed, the love song my ex-spouse and I received as a wedding gift immortalized the very beginnings of our love, not its future. Its nostalgic lyrics recalled our meet-cute, a divine spark that promised a happily ever after. Its protagonists were two people so infatuated they would drive all night or fly across an ocean to be with each other. They weren't preparing to grow old together, nor learning to repair the cracks between them to make something stronger and more resilient.

It's a beautiful song and a beautiful story, but the truth is more complicated and not as pretty. For a long time, I let that beautiful story stop me from facing the reality of my marriage or talking openly about how hard some aspects of it were. I was afraid that if I did, I would lose the parts of our love that I cherished and the home we had made together. I was afraid to find out who I would become if I stopped being my spouse's wife.

"Failing at our marriage feels scarier than starting over alone," read one of my journal entries from that time. I was afraid of what other people would think of me for failing so publicly. I believed in our love story, and I wanted it to be true. Yet, in the end, I couldn't hinge my future on something that felt most natural in front of an audience.

In some ways, the realest that marriage ever felt to me was when I got divorced. I was eight months into a mandatory year-long separation from my spouse (a condition of getting divorced in BC) when the US legalized same-sex marriage in June 2015. My social media feed was all rainbow flags and shiny new engagement rings. "I'm so over gay marriage," I texted the only other queer divorced person I knew. "Gay divorce is so hot right now!" we snarked, though in truth I felt like an outlier, not a trendsetter.

At the time, I wondered if all those newly engaged queer people fully understood what they were getting themselves into. Marriage is an institution symbolically associated with permanence, fidelity, and a shared dedication to working things out.[30] Being legally bound to another person also makes it harder to leave them. Would some of us have made different choices if marriage equality campaigns had spent a fraction of their millions on public service announcements aimed at educating us on the legal, financial, and social ramifications of divorce?

I wish someone had told me to read the fine print before I signed my marriage licence. We made our wedding as queer as possible, but our breakup was on the government's terms. Getting divorced took more than a year, required reams of paperwork, and cost thousands of dollars in legal fees. I gobbled up my swirl cone of romance and pragmatism, but the institution left a bad taste in my mouth.

It's been almost eight years since I last talked to my ex-spouse. My silence wasn't a conscious decision so much as a slow fading away of my efforts to sustain a friendship after our divorce. For a time, I wanted to be the kind of person who could stay friends with my ex. It seemed to fulfill another stereotypical queer relationship narrative, the one where you go from exes to besties. Was I a less emotionally evolved person for not being able to stay friends with my ex-spouse? Had I again failed at delivering the ending that was expected of me?

Today I believe in the power of writing new narratives and of letting go of the constraints we place on what our relationships should look like, including when they end or take on a different shape. I still cry at weddings, but I won't get married again. I want to love expansively and bind my life to the people I'm committed to because I trust that we're in it together, in all of our beautiful mess.

The Beginning After the End

I had grown used to my bare ring finger by the time my divorce was finalized, though I still occasionally experienced the phantom sensation of my missing jewellery, reflexively searching for something that wasn't there. What once burned now felt haunted.

I needed a ritual to exorcise the ghosts of my marriage. I took my wedding and engagement rings out of the jewellery box where they had been sitting for months and cleansed them in a shallow dish of water charged under a full moon.

Using a pair of kitchen scissors as a makeshift magical tool, I symbolically cut any remaining ties between me and my ex-spouse. My aim was to unbind us in the hope that we both might feel freer. When I was finished, I put my rings in a small muslin bag with a nickel-sized piece of pale-pink rose quartz shaped like a lopsided heart with a nick at its centre. It reminded me of my own soft, strong heart, still beating despite its scars. I was beginning to see who I could become after wife. I liked what I saw.

I tucked the bag with the rings into my jewellery box, then poured the moon-charged water into a plastic container. I walked the few blocks from my apartment to the community hall where I was married. The weathered green wood and stucco exterior looked the same, as did the grey-painted stairs where I once stood as a bride. I pictured my younger self, so hopeful and self-assured. I wished I could brace her for the grief and heartache to come. I wanted her to know that someday, she would find a love that felt easy, where she wouldn't have to try so hard.

I pulled the water from my pocket, cupping the small round vessel in my left hand. Through the plastic, the cool liquid felt soothing in my palm. Glancing around to make sure no one was watching, I poured the moon-charged water into the soil beneath the building's cedar hedge, certain the earth could hold whatever had washed from my rings.

I trusted that there was more to my story than a happily ever after.

I cast a spell that whatever I poured into the soil that day might help it grow.

BETWEEN WORLDS

RECENT DIVORCÉE seeks hot mascs for playful fun; bonus points for switches with capable hands. Horny for intimacy, connection, and people with primary partners. Still licking my wounds. If you're lucky, I'll let you lick them too.

Riley and I sat on the sun-warmed wooden stoop of a small utility cabin, our bodies as close as we could get without touching. The electric current of lust between us shot sparks whenever I accidentally-on-purpose bumped my leg into theirs.

We were at a week-long witchcamp near a BC mountain lake. After the ritual last night, I was bold enough to confess I had twice dreamt about kissing them. Why did I feel so shy now that we were planning to do it in real life?

"I have a partner named Mia," said Riley. "I checked in with them before witchcamp. They're okay with us hooking up." We were partway through a conversation about our relationship statuses, sexual health needs, and desires.

"You did?" I asked, blushing.

"Yeah," they said with a grin. "There was a vibe."

I grinned back. Maybe I wasn't the only one having premonitions.

I didn't realize my attraction to Riley had been so obvious when we ran into each other a month before camp. It wasn't just that they were masculine, athletic, and a half-inch taller than me. Riley seemed like someone who would organize a game of capture-the-flag in the morning, repair a friend's bike in the afternoon, then cook me dinner and send me home with leftovers. I wondered what else they could do with those capable hands.

"Oh, and I might be pregnant," Riley added, interrupting my reverie. "I've had a known donor's sperm in me recently, in case that's helpful to know."

Noticing the surprise on my face, they quickly explained that they were planning to co-parent with a close friend, Mars, and Mars's partner, Nic. Their partner Mia would be part of their family, too, but not in a core parenting role. The foursome, who had already visited a few smaller communities, hoped to someday leave the city to live more rurally.

I was intrigued by Riley's intention to parent with multiple people—all of the queer parents I knew were married or co-parenting with an ex—but it didn't seem relevant to my future plans. I had just started dating again and was leery of commitment. I wasn't ready to be anyone's wife or girlfriend, let alone a mom.

"It's cool you're doing that," I said, "and also pretty different from where I'm at. I'm happily single and I don't want kids. You have a partner and are trying to have a baby with two other people. How about we keep this thing between us a camp romance?"

"What happens at witchcamp stays at witchcamp?" asked Riley.

"What happens at witchcamp stays at witchcamp."

In the distance, late-August sunlight glinted off the surface of the lake, almost as if the water were winking at us.

I looked sideways at Riley, smiling wolfishly, my crooked eyetooth poking out like a fang. "You know, I've never had sex with a pregnant person before. This could be my chance. Want to chase each other through the woods after sunset?"

Now it was Riley's turn to blush.

> **CRUSHED-OUT GEMINI** seeks earthy Taurus to watch me draw imaginary graphs about falling in love. You bring your laser pointer, I'll wear nothing but my heart on my sleeve.

It was the winter solstice—the longest night of the year. The cherry trees outside my bedroom window shivered in the late-December chill. Like me, they were naked, having long since shed the last of their leaves as autumn turned to winter. I burrowed deeper into the sheets, pulling the duvet up to my chin. My mother had given me flannel pyjamas every year for Christmas until she got too sick to shop for presents. These pistachio-coloured flannel sheets were the first thing I bought after leaving my marriage.

My bedding was one of the only things I kept with me through a year of living in other people's apartments. I had moved into my own place a month ago, finally ready to commit to at least one kind of permanence. My new home was all flawless white surfaces with pops of pink, green, and gold, a femme haven one friend likened to being inside an iPhone. To me, it was proof I could walk away from everything and rise again.

Riley dozed on the pillow beside me, lulled into a post-sex slumber. What happened at witchcamp *hadn't* stayed at witchcamp. With Mia's blessing, we had been seeing each other since September. Riley wasn't pregnant yet, but our crush was nearing the end of its first trimester. At camp, the witches leading our nightly rituals often said, "What happens between worlds changes all of the worlds." Had Riley and I accidentally cast a love spell by hooking up in a magical portal?

Riley's eyes blinked open. "Did I fall asleep?" they asked, yawning.

I reached over to run my fingers through their sandy-brown curls. They relaxed into my touch, butting against my palm like a cat. "You seemed tired, so I didn't wake you. Anyway, you don't have to rush home tonight."

We typically saw each other once a week and were having a special two-night date ahead of Riley's trip to Toronto to spend the holidays with a friend. It was the most time we'd spent together since witchcamp.

"Happy solstice, baby," Riley said.

"Happy solstice. I'm glad I get to spend tonight with you."

"Let's go to the beach tomorrow morning to watch the sunrise."

We kissed, an impromptu blessing for the longest night of the year.

I paused, gathering the courage to say the words I'd been scripting in my head while they slept. "So I've been wondering ... If you were on a trajectory of falling in love with me—say, like this"—I stopped to trace a line in the air with my finger—"and I was on a trajectory of falling in love with you"—I drew another almost parallel line beside it—"where would we both be on this trajectory?"

I looked awfully serious for a naked woman drawing an imaginary graph over her bed.

"Zena, I love you," Riley said, with the certainty of a triple earth sign.

"You do?" I said, suddenly shy. "I love you too!"

Then I was crying into Riley's armpit, hiding my face as a shield against the vulnerability of saying those words. Riley pulled me in closer. I let them hold me, my resistance melting away in the press of our bodies.

Losing my mom and my marriage in the same year had armoured my heart. With Riley, all of my softest parts felt exposed. Wanting them was fun. Saying "I love you" was like admitting I needed them. That scared me. Was it too risky to let myself fall for someone whose dreams of the future were so different? What did *I* want? I had been in survival mode for so long that imagining my future was like looking into a mirror smeared with petroleum jelly. Could I be brave enough to trust Riley with my wary, yearning heart?

PUSH MY BUTTONS AND LET'S SEE WHERE IT TAKES US. I might cry, but at least it will be an interesting ride.

It was a rainy Friday evening in March. Riley had picked me up from work for our weekly date, sparing me the soggy bus ride home. Their car was a warm, dry haven from Vancouver's dreary streets, where cars sped through puddles, soaking unwary pedestrians. Riley drove with a cyclist's care, never losing sight of how they might be sharing the road with someone whose body was softer and less protected.

We were on our way to my place for dinner. Riley took pleasure in cooking for us and had come prepared with a cloth shopping bag bursting with ingredients: delicate yellow squash from their garden, sausages from a local farmer they bought from in bulk, a nutty rice blend. They were an instinctive cook, remixing every recipe they came across, while I tended to hew strictly to the rules. Content to be their lead dish-doer and occasional sous-chef, I took pleasure in watching them take command of my kitchen.

Riley pulled into my building's underground garage, where they parked their battered grey compact car. Affectionately known as the Mouse, it had a broken door handle and a tape deck we mostly used to listen to the *Dirty Dancing* soundtrack. We grabbed the groceries and our work stuff from the back seat and caught the elevator to my third-floor apartment.

With its green-and-gold faux marble walls, oak veneer railing, and scuffed brass-finish hardware, the elevator looked like a time machine that went exclusively to the early nineties. I jabbed the 3 button on the number panel. It didn't light up anymore, so I was in the habit of pressing it extra hard, as if to grab the machine's attention.

I let out a satisfied sigh as the elevator lurched into motion.

"I didn't have time for lunch today," said Riley, who was leaning against the wall with an oversized messenger bag slung over their shoulder. They worked at a cycling non-profit and had spent the afternoon teaching sixth graders the fundamentals of bike safety. "I'm hungry!"

My shoulders tensed as I scanned the perimeter of the small, square box. We were the only people in the elevator. Why did it suddenly feel smaller?

"What's happening for you right now?" asked Riley, noticing my changed bearing.

"I think I just time travelled."

Riley tilted their head inquiringly. "Say more?"

I explained how my ex sometimes acted like it was my fault they hadn't eaten all day, even if we had been apart for ten hours. Most of my homecomings were peaceful enough, but I couldn't predict when I'd open the door to an avalanche of blame.

"I thought you were going to get mad at me. It's not logical, I know."

"I'm an adult. It's not your responsibility to make sure I eat," Riley said, enfolding me in a hug. I relaxed into their chest, my tears soaking the embroidered flower on the "Slowly but Surely" patch sewn to their brown-wool jacket.

"You're so nice to me. Why am I always crying on you?" I laughed through my tears. Riley chuckled, holding me a little closer.

My friend Vivenne's words, both prophecy and promise, came back to me as the elevator juddered to a stop on my floor.

"It's going to hurt," she'd told me the previous winter over FaceTime from her Toronto bedroom. Flanked by overstuffed bookshelves and a row of stilettos, she doled out hard-won femme wisdom while waving a copy of *Codependent No More* at me. "When you finally meet someone who loves you like you need to be loved, it's going to hurt."

Loving Riley was easy—easier than I had ever known love could be—but that didn't make it simple. Old bruises sat just beneath the surface of my skin, invisible even to me until moments like this one that pressed right into the heart of a wound.

I LOVE NOT CAMPING BUT I'LL SLEEP IN A TENT FOR YOU. City femme seeks outdoorsy companions for forest adventures. I'll bring the marshmallows.

Nic and Mars assembled their tent on the opposite side of our campsite with the practised rhythms of a couple who had done this many times. Mars, wearing a light cotton shirt over their curves to protect their fair, freckled skin from burning, hummed an old folk song as they hammered in tent pegs. Nic surveyed the site, her eyes like calculators as she strategized where to hang our rain and shade tarps. With her army-green brimmed sun hat, brown-plaid button-up, and sturdy build, she could easily have been mistaken for a lesbian park ranger.

It was an unseasonably cold weekend in July, so we were preparing for sun, rain, and anything else a West Coast summer might throw our way. I made a silent wish for warm, dry weather. The luggage tag on my suitcase at home declared, "I love not camping." Witchcamp was a notable exception to my no-camping policy. So was this weekend, the first trip I'd ever taken with Riley, Nic, and Mars. I didn't understand the allure of sleeping in a tent when hotels across BC had perfectly comfortable beds for rent, but I was trying to be a team player.

"Hey, can you help me put the fly on?" Riley called from where they were pitching our two-person tent beside a mossy stump. We had put as much distance as possible between the tents for privacy and as a buffer against the sound of Mars's snoring. I needed quiet. Grieving had made me an uneasy sleeper.

"Nice and cozy," I said after we finished putting it up, admiring the comfortable nest of pillows and sleeping bags we'd made. If I had to spend three nights in a tent, at least Riley and I would be snuggled together like squirrels in a nest.

Nic and Mars sat sipping on chilled cans of cider at the weathered wooden picnic table that doubled as our kitchen and dining area. I grabbed a family-sized bag of plain ripple chips and headed over.

"What's that?" I asked, pointing at the board game sitting in front of Nic. I took a handful of chips, then passed the bag across the table to Mars. Riley sat down beside me, grazing on a bag of white-cheddar popcorn as they cracked open a can of IPA.

"It's called Forbidden Desert," Nic said, her Australian accent drawing out the vowels. "We're a team of adventurers trying to escape a sandstorm by reassembling an ancient flying machine. We have to work together to win." A games enthusiast and patient teacher, she arrayed colourful game tiles, markers, and cards on the table as she carefully explained the rules.

Board game instructions usually sounded like the teacher on *A Charlie Brown Christmas* to me, the words dissolving into wah-wah trombone noises. I resisted the urge to tune Nic out. This weekend was too important for me to keep sliding into old habits. Nic and Mars were some of the most significant people in Riley's life. We had been friendly for several years in the way queers who go to the same house parties are, but we weren't close. Since Riley and I were still in our "spend as much of our twenty-four-hour dates as possible in bed" era, we hadn't hung out with Nic and Mars very often since we started dating. This camping trip was a chance for us to get to know each other better. I wanted them to like me.

"So how are things going with you guys?" Mars asked, smiling warmly across the table at Riley and me. Was I imagining the flicker of concern in their blue eyes?

The four of us were thrust into a new kind of intimacy in April when Riley and Mia broke up. Riley had phoned to tell me from the driveway of the suburban three-bedroom townhouse they were readying to move into with Nic and Mars.

"We're good," answered Riley. "Still figuring things out."

I nodded, giving their thigh a reassuring squeeze under the picnic table.

"Yeah, still figuring things out," I added. "It's a lot to think about."

After the breakup, Riley and I paused to ask ourselves what our relationship could be now that it had room to grow. We both wanted more than a weekly date, but we didn't know exactly what that meant.

When Riley and Mia were still together, I told myself that Riley could never be my capital-P partner because I didn't want children—or the added complication of two co-parents I hardly knew and who hardly knew me. Riley's family and their future plans seemed like a closed circle. I felt safer on the outside, alone with Riley in our own little bubble.

The thing about bubbles is that they're bound to pop eventually. Did I want to build something more permanent with Riley, Nic, and Mars? Could I change my mind about wanting kids? Would Mars and Nic be open to parenting with me if I did? We all had to agree for this plan to work. It's one thing to play at rebuilding an imaginary flying machine. Raising a child together was a whole other kind of teamwork, one I wasn't sure I was ready for.

I looked over at our tents. Having more than two people inside them would be too crowded for me. Together, they were just right, spaced closely enough to feel connected, with plenty of room between them so that it didn't seem like the walls between us were collapsing.

I thought of how bubbles sometimes formed new shapes by sticking together. Maybe I needed to stay in a bubble with Riley a little longer, gradually floating nearer to Mars and Nic to see if we could stick together and create something new.

DO THEY MAKE TRAINING WHEELS FOR FEELINGS?
Recovering codependent and aspiring cyclist still wobbling as I learn how to let you need me. I promise to love you wholeheartedly but I'm gonna crash into you sometimes.

It was a warm afternoon in early September. The armpits of my lightweight black cardigan were damp with sweat. I flapped my arms like a chicken, trying to generate a breeze. "How do I look?" I asked Riley, fussing with the belt on my sundress as they manoeuvred the Mouse into a narrow parking space on a block filled with expensive cars.

"You look great," said Riley. "Aren't you hot in that sweater, though?"

"Yeah, but it's my first time meeting your aunts, uncles, and cousins. Look at this place," I said, gesturing to the stately brick home that was our destination. "It's fancy! I want to look nice, not all scabby."

I had matching gashes on each arm from falling during a lesson with Riley, who was teaching me to ride a bike. After weeks of coasting back and forth in crooked lines, I was so proud of pedalling in circles around an elementary school basketball court. Next thing I knew, I was on the asphalt, my legs tangled in the spokes, elbows oozing blood and dirt.

"Are you nervous?" asked Riley.

I nodded. "Aren't you?"

"No, they're going to love you."

Riley and I had been dating for a year but had only been presenting more publicly as a couple for a few months. Having already gained and lost one set of in-laws, meeting Riley's extended family carried a particular significance for me.

Riley winced as they reached over to unbuckle their seat belt.

"Is your back sore? Do you need an ibuprofen?"

"Yeah, sure." Riley smiled their thanks as I gave them a painkiller and a bottle of water from my purse.

We had just gotten back from our second witchcamp together. If last year had been about casting a love spell, this year confronted us with the reality that we would sometimes find ourselves lying side by side in the dark, unreachable.

Riley's back went out soon after we arrived for the week-long camp. Moving hurt. Breathing hurt. Everything hurt. It was like the colour and volume had been turned down on the version of them I remembered from last year, a moonlit satyr as insatiable as I was.

"I keep thinking back to that night in the tent," said Riley, their eyes on the windshield.

I winced, remembering how I froze as they cried beside me, immobilized by pain. They needed me to say something comforting or turn on a flashlight to help pull them out of a spiral. Instead of tossing them a rope, I lay there silently, unable to drag myself out of the quicksand of my resistance. Asphyxiated by need, I couldn't take care of anyone but myself.

"It was lonely having you right there and still so far away," said Riley, their eyes welling with tears. "It makes it harder to ask you for help."

Like me, Riley had a habit of swallowing their needs, more at ease in the role of caregiver than care receiver. Yet while they were flooded with feelings in moments like that night in the tent, I tended to shut down, turning to stone.

"I know. I'm sorry I wasn't there when you needed me."

My stomach churned, acid with guilt. I wanted Riley to trust that I would be there for them and to feel as safe with me as I did with them. I was waking up to just how much hurt and anger I still carried from years of swallowing my own needs to care for my dying mother and my ex-spouse. A tangled ball of old resentments was lodged inside me like hair in a drain.

What would it take to get it out, and how could I protect Riley from getting splashed by all the muck it dredged up?

COMING OUT OF MY SHELL. Let's show our soft underbellies by the ocean.

The Pacific Ocean lapped at the beach, tossing its treasures onto the pebbled shore: hunks of driftwood, their edges worn smooth by water; sheafs of seaweed; blackberry brambles knotted around sinewy tree branches; an empty red rock crab shell, the tiny feelers still attached.

Riley and I were the only people on the beach that overcast October afternoon. The wind whipped our curls in the air as we walked along the water's edge, balancing on washed-up logs as we headed toward the granite boulder with the widest view of the ocean. Following along behind Riley as they scrambled up the massive rock, I found footholds between grooves filled with seawater, each one a habitat for grey-and-beige crabs no bigger than my thumbnail.

At the top, we sat huddled against the autumn chill, watching the wind ripple across the water. "Puppyhead!" I called out when I saw a slick black seal head pop out from under the surface, its big-eyed, whiskered face reminiscent of a friendly dog's.

I rested my head on Riley's shoulder, nuzzling into the warmth of their coat.

"I've been thinking about us," said Riley. "I know we're not ready yet, but I want to live with you someday. I want to be part of a family with you."

"I want that too. I sometimes wonder what it would be like to live with you, Nic, Mars, and a kid. When I picture it, we're not in the city anymore. It's weirdly not impossible to imagine."

"Weirdly not impossible?" Riley laughed.

"You know what I mean."

"I do. I've been talking to Nic and Mars about it too. They're curious to know how you might fit into our future plans—especially Mars. I think the uncertainty is harder for them."

While I'd been warming to the idea of co-parenting, I was hesitant to talk about the future with Nic and Mars, fearful I might feel pressured to make a commitment I wasn't ready for. Riley had become our reluctant go-between, offering reassurances on both sides.

"I love you so much," I said. "And I sometimes get scared that by saying yes to all this I'm bending myself to fit someone else's dreams. I don't want to lose you, but that can't be the reason we stay together."

"I don't want to lose you either, or to push you into something you don't want. I just wish I didn't feel so stuck in the middle between you, Nic, and Mars."

Seagulls called overhead as we sat quietly with our eyes trained on the waves. Everything around us was liquid. I scanned the horizon, searching for solid land.

After sunset, Riley and I soaked naked in the hot tub on their parents' deck. We could hear the tide coming in. A crescent moon was just visible behind the clouds.

"I feel like a turtle," I said, sunk down deep enough that only my head was visible above the water. "Too many big feelings today. I want to hide in my shell."

"Come here," said Riley, reaching for me. I resisted at first, then relaxed into their embrace. The hot water loosened my limbs as they cradled me, rocking slowly back and forth.

Tears pressed at the corners of my eyes. I clamped down to staunch the flow, as if clutching a remaining shard of my outer shell. Then I pictured my mother watching over us from a corner of the night sky, sure of how glad she would be to see me loved with such tenderness.

I let the tears come.

I CAN'T SEE THE FUTURE, BUT I CAN SEE A FUTURE WITH YOU. Let's gaze into a crystal ball together and find out what happens next.

I sat cross-legged on an oversized cushion in our teacher Sofia's living room, using my right thigh as a makeshift table for my black hardcover journal. Riley was sprawled nearby on a navy-blue velvet couch by the wood stove, writing in a fat red notebook. We were on Salt Spring Island for a weekend-long workshop led by a witch we knew from camp. There were around twenty of us scattered around the room. It was quiet except for the sounds of pens scratching on paper, the fire crackling in the background.

Sofia's house was perched on a ridge with a view of arbutus and Douglas fir trees. I glanced out the window and saw an eagle gliding on a warm current of air high above the treetops. It made me think of my mother, to whom eagles were sacred. Her birthday was a few days away. The third anniversary of her death was last month. Spring, a season traditionally associated with new beginnings, had become a time of grieving for me. I recalled how skinless I was three years ago, how bereft. My grief felt softer now. Had time rubbed smooth its roughest edges?

I looked down at my journal, where, earlier in the day, I had drawn my life as a river. It curved diagonally across the page, the dense cluster of dots in 2014 and 2015 staring back at me like proof of everything I had lost.

"I want you to imagine yourselves ten years from now," Sofia said from her place by the hearth. A seasoned ritualist, her voice had the resonance of a cello. I closed my eyes as she guided us through visualizing the future, my weight settling in the bowl of my pelvis as I imagined myself growing roots that stretched far into earth. Where would I be in 2027? It was hard enough to imagine where I'd be a year from now, in the spring of 2018.

I snuck a peek at Riley, who was lying beside the couch with both hands on their belly. Their face was placid, though the tiny furrow in their brow signalled deep concentration. *I'll bet they're calling in a baby*, I thought as I watched them rub their abdomen in gentle circles. After a break from trying, Riley had started inseminating again in January. Each month since had been a dance of hope and disappointment. I felt guilty for not being as devastated as they were every time they found out their latest attempt had failed.

Having a child was Riley's lifelong dream, not mine. I used to be so certain I would never become a parent. I had my whole future mapped out, and it didn't include kids. I held fast to this idea, even after parts of the map were erased by loss. Falling in love with Riley landed me in entirely new terrain. My life was suddenly full of possibilities—and a lot of unknowns. What if I said yes to co-parenting with Riley, Mars, and Nic and realized I had made a mistake? What if I said no and lost everything?

My reticence to commit to a shared vision of the future had become an unspoken point of tension between Mars and me. They wanted to know how I would fit into their plans with Nic and Riley and what role I would play in their child's life. I wanted the freedom to change my mind.

But was it really freedom I was after, or was I trying to insulate myself against loss? The truth was, I *wanted* a family. Not the get-married-white-picket-fence kind—I'd tried that one, and it ended in a spectacular failure. I didn't want a diamond ring. I wanted to trust that I could rely on other people to take care of me and to know that they could rely on me too.

I didn't want to be a wife or a mother, but I also didn't want fear to be the thing that kept me from Riley, Nic, and Mars, or for it to stop me from having a relationship with their child. "I'm not alone. I have a family," I wrote in my journal. "I know how to find my way home."

WE'RE HAVING A BABY. You pee on a stick, I'll celebrate with you. We can figure out the rest later.

An early morning breeze whispered through my windows, cooling the air around me as I washed my breakfast dishes. It would be muggy outside by the time I left for the office. I pictured myself wilting in the July heat on an un-air-conditioned bus, then imagined Riley waking for a morning swim. They were at a lakeside lodge an hour outside the city for the summer, working as the director of a camp for kids with cancer.

Riley lived there almost full-time, so we only saw each other every couple of weeks.

I glanced at my phone, checking the time. It was just after 6:00 a.m., so Riley was probably still in bed. Just then, my phone pinged with a notification—a Facebook message from Riley, who didn't have cell service at camp. I opened their message and saw a photograph of a positive pregnancy test accompanied by ten crying-face emojis. "That's me joy crying," they wrote, "though honestly I don't know if I believe it yet." It was their first positive pregnancy test in almost two years of trying.

"BABYYYYYYYYYYYYYYYY! I'm so happy for you," I texted back. "OMG A BABY LET'S DO THIS."

Dishes abandoned, I stood in my kitchen exchanging excited messages with Riley. They had already shared the news by email with Mars and Nic, who were on a road trip through Atlantic Canada. Riley planned to visit their doctor for a blood test the next time they were in the city. They wanted definitive proof that this pregnancy was real.

"Can't words. So many swirly thoughts and feels," they wrote.

"You don't need to find the words. Just be in the moment."

We made plans to celebrate on Friday night when Riley was home for the weekend. We had been exchanging messages for almost forty-five minutes, so we started saying our goodbyes. They were on their way to get a cup of tea and watch the kids go for a Rip 'n' Dip—camp lingo for an early swim.

"I love you, Zena. You've been such a rock on this journey, and it's starting in a whole new way now. So shocked for real."

"I love you!" I replied. "I can't wait to celebrate with you (and zygote). BABY I'M SO EXCITED FOR YOU / US / THE FAMILY!"

After Riley signed off, I sank down onto the grey tile floor to reread their first message, squinting to see the faint blue lines on the pregnancy test. How did I feel about their news now that the prospect of having a child together had become a reality? I closed my eyes and felt fireworks dancing inside. *I want this baby.* I still wasn't sure what parenting would look like for me, but I was ready to find out. A knot of worry I didn't know I had been holding unclenched as I allowed myself to trust in the fact of my desire.

PARENTING IS A TEAM SPORT AND I DON'T WANT TO BE IN CHARGE. Can I be your co-captain?

The midwifery clinic had a homey feel, with worn checkerboard linoleum floors, a lounge decorated with mismatched sofas and thrifted chairs, and a bulletin board papered with baby photos and community event posters. Riley, Mars, Nic, and I sat in a loose circle with a dozen other expectant parents. Nic—an extroverted introvert—struck up a conversation with the dad beside her while Mars sipped from a mug of herbal tea to ward off the January chill. The four of us had recently rung in 2018 together. I could hardly believe that in only a few months, we would meet our child.

Riley's jeans had a wide black band of stretchy fabric to accommodate their ever-expanding belly. They pulled a roll of antacid from their pocket.

"Heartburn?" I asked.

"Yeah, party fish is squishing my organs again."

"More like party shark," I quipped.

"Welcome, everyone!" said the instructor, a russet-haired white woman with fine black floral tattoos peeking out from under her V-neck T-shirt. "I'm Misha, and I'm honoured to be leading today's prenatal-in-a-day class. Let's get started with a round of introductions."

As we went around the circle, I noticed that most of the pregnant people had only one person accompanying them, usually a partner. Our four-parent family was an anomaly, even at a class taught by a queer doula in one of the city's most queer- and trans-friendly midwifery clinics.

"Hi, I'm Riley. I'm thirty weeks pregnant, and I'm here with my partner, Zena, and my co-parents, Mars and Nic. The four of us will be raising our baby together."

"That sounds like a great adult-to-child ratio," said Misha. A few other expectant parents nodded in agreement, a hungry look in their eyes.

"I'm Mars. I'm one of Riley's co-parents. I'll be supporting them during labour and will have a lead parenting role in our family."

Riley's pregnancy was the motivation we needed to finally start talking about the practicalities of parenting. We had recently started using the language of "lead parent" and "vice-parent" to describe our roles. The main difference was that Riley and Mars would carry a greater share of the parenting responsibilities, like waking up with the baby at night and doing more of the everyday care.

"I'm Nic, also on Team Riley."

"And I'm Zena. Nic and I are the vice-parents. We'll be at the birth too and will be part of our baby's care, just not as much as Riley and Mars." Was that too much information? I was still getting used to explaining our family to strangers.

One thing I knew for sure was that being a vice-parent felt right to me. I was excited to have a significant role in our baby's life, but I planned to keep my apartment, splitting my time between there and the family townhouse. I wasn't ready to give up my home, and I liked the idea of taking breaks from what would soon be an even fuller house.

I flipped open my pocket-sized pink notebook as Misha ran through what we'd cover in class. The first page was dated September 27, 2012, the day I flew to Thunder Bay to see my dying mother after not coming home for two years. I'd unwittingly grabbed the same notebook I had used to record my mother's funeral wishes. "I'm not afraid of dying," she'd said. "I'm afraid of being buried in the wrong place." The page after it was blank.

I turned the page again, needing a thicker buffer between birth and death.

We didn't bury my mother's ashes until the spring of 2016. She had been dead for two years. At her interment, strangers kept telling me, "You look just like your mother." I stayed up late after the memorial wondering if I should have a child. Did I owe my mother a descendant?

Now, almost two years later, I was preparing to give her one, though not in a way either of us could have imagined while she was alive. I knew from reading my mother's journals that she had hoped I might someday become a mother too. Her death put me on a queerer path to parenthood. The baby Riley was carrying would be my mother's grandchild. It didn't matter that they weren't related by blood or DNA.

We were bound together by love and the courage to risk creating something new.

KNEE-DEEP IN THE PASSENGER SEAT AND I'M FREAKING YOU OUT. Is it casual now?

Two thoughts competed for my attention as I steered the small boxy black SUV out of my building's underground parkade: *Why is that concrete wall coming at us so quickly?* and *OH SHIT!*

I slammed on the brakes. The seat belt pulled taut across my torso as the car lurched abruptly to a stop two inches from the wall. Beside me in the passenger seat, Riley had one hand braced on the dashboard and the other wrapped protectively around their abdomen. I couldn't tell if they were breathing heavily because I'd almost crashed the car, or they were having a contraction, or both.

"Are you okay?" I said.

Riley nodded, the rosy pregnant glow in their cheeks gone paper white.

"I'm so sorry!" I said, my mouth screwed into a grimace. I resisted the urge to say more. I knew if I kept apologizing I would fall further into the shame spiral I was trying to claw myself out of. I didn't want Riley, who I was there to care of, to feel like they had to take care of me.

It was a sunny Saturday afternoon in March. Riley and I had spent the morning walking along the beach at an East Vancouver park where cargo ships dotted our ocean view. I stopped to take a photo of Riley cradling their belly beside a fallen tree bleached white by salt and sun, the North Shore Mountains in the distance, the sky behind them a vibrant baby blue.

We were in the elevator on our way back to my apartment when their water broke. TV shows had trained me to expect a dramatic gush of liquid hitting the floor, but instead it was Riley staring down at their denim-clad crotch, saying, "I think my water just broke?"

They phoned their midwife, who told Riley it would be hours before they were in active labour, so we didn't need to hurry. Since they planned to give birth at home, we stayed at my apartment until Riley's contractions got intense enough that they knew it was time to go. I volunteered to drive us to their townhouse. An anxious driver, especially on highways, I was feigning the confidence I needed to make the half-hour trip to the suburbs in the boxy grey SUV Riley shared with Nic and Mars.

I guess I wasn't faking hard enough. We hadn't even made it out of the garage yet.

I looked over at Riley, who was leaning back in the passenger seat with their eyes closed. The light sheen of sweat on their forehead told me they were having another contraction.

I took a deep breath, stretching my fingers to loosen my chokehold on the steering wheel. Double-checking to make sure I had the car in the right gear, I reversed away from the wall, slowly piloting the SUV up the ramp leading out of the garage.

I can do this, I told myself, scanning the alley for bikes and pedestrians before carefully pulling out of the driveway, then turning right.

No, you can't! another voice inside me shouted.

I managed to get halfway around the block before pulling to a stop in front of my building.

"I can't do this," I said, crying. I put the car in park and turned off the ignition. "It's not safe."

"It's okay," said Riley, with the preternatural calm of someone whose body was being overtaken by a primal force. "Let's phone Ollie to see if they can drive us." We had tickets to see a movie matinee later that afternoon with Riley's best friend, who lived nearby. Ollie was part of Riley's birth support team and would be Uncle Ollie to the baby.

As we sat waiting for our rescuer to arrive, I silently chastised myself for not being calmer. This wasn't who I wanted to be today. When I had imagined Riley's birth, I pictured myself mopping their brow and letting them squeeze my hand until my finger bones crunched, as stoic as a devoted father-to-be with a femme's emotional intelligence.

My romantic fantasies didn't include losing my shit in a Honda CRV and almost crashing into a concrete wall. A barrage of unanswered questions jostled for my attention. Who would Riley and I be to each other once we were no longer just partners but co-parents? Would our baby's birth mean the death of our love? How would I fit into the family we were making? Would I be a good enough parent? Did I even know how to take care of a baby? I wanted to trust that everything would work out, but everything suddenly felt so uncertain. It scared me.

Our whole lives were about to change, and I wasn't in control anymore—birth was. I was beginning to understand just how powerful a force of transformation it could be.

SURE, FISTING IS COOL, BUT CAN YOU PUSH AN ENTIRE HUMAN OUT OF YOUR BODY? Awestruck femme ready to cheer you on while you work your magic from the inside out.

Our midwife coached Riley through the final stages of pushing, their eyes radiating kindness through their glasses. "Breathe in and bear down," they said, counting down the seconds until it was time for Riley to exhale. "Gently. That's it. You're doing great. We're almost there."

We had caravanned to the hospital on Sunday at sunrise when our midwife determined that Riley needed fluids and more pain relief options than were available at home. They were exhausted and dehydrated from being in labour for more than twenty-four hours. I felt a wash of gratitude when the colour returned to Riley's cheeks after an anesthesiologist in crisp maroon scrubs and a teddy bear–print surgical cap gave them an epidural.

When it came time to push, Mars and Ollie stood on either side of the hospital bed, each bracing one of Riley's bent legs. Nic, our designated photographer, snapped photos. I stood near Riley's head, whispering encouragements, until our midwife signalled that it was time for Mars to catch the baby. I took Mars's place at Riley's leg.

The baby emerged in glimpses. We saw her red hair, wet and matted, then her tiny, scrunched newborn face as Riley breathed through the intensity of freeing her head and shoulders. With a final mighty push, she surged into Mars's waiting hands, her body still attached to Riley's by a pulsing umbilical cord.

"Riley, your baby's huge!" Ollie exclaimed.

I thought so too, but she turned out to be a fairly average seven pounds. The immensity of her arrival fooled our eyes. Birth, the ultimate magic trick. All five of us—Riley, Nic, Mars, Ollie, and me—burst into tears when we saw Sasha. She cried, and we cried with her, a tiny traveller tasting oxygen for the first time as she arrived home to meet her family.

DO YOU BELIEVE IN LOVE AT FIRST SIGHT? I didn't until I met you.

I showed up at Riley, Mars, and Nic's townhouse on Monday morning with a coffee in one hand and a freshly bought nursing bra in the other. "I'll find the most gender-neutral one I can," I promised Riley, who hadn't had a chance to buy one before they went into labour. The best I could do was a heather-grey sports bra devoid of lace or bows.

Our daughter, whom we had decided to call Sasha, wasn't yet a day old. She had spent every hour of her life cradled in someone's arms, with Riley, Mars, and Nic spelling off throughout her first night. I was the only one who still hadn't held her. I loved Sasha from the moment she took her first breath, but yesterday at the hospital I couldn't make myself ask to take her from Riley's arms. She didn't feel like mine. Was I a parent, or a trespasser?

I had been awake for almost twenty-four hours by the time I took a cab home from the hospital last night. Mars and Nic stayed with Riley and the baby to wait for Riley's epidural to wear off before driving back to the townhouse. As they took turns rocking our newborn, I slept alone in my apartment. The blaring of a car alarm jarred me awake after midnight. I had woken up sweaty and disoriented, heart pounding with adrenalin as I sat blinking in the dark, trying to comprehend that I had a daughter.

I felt a sense of homecoming as I walked up the path to the townhouse and saw Riley sitting in the rocking chair by the window with Sasha cradled in their arms. She was born several days after the fourth anniversary of my mother's death. No longer just a season of loss, spring had become a season of birth for me too. I thought back to last April, when I sat in Sofia's living room trying to conjure where I would be in ten years. "I'm not alone. I have a family," I had written then. "I know how to find my way home."

I let myself in without knocking, softly calling out a hello as I hung my raincoat in the hall closet. I crept quietly up the stairs, trying not to wake Mars and Nic, who were in their bedroom sleeping off a wakeful night.

Riley and Sasha's faces were illuminated by sunlight filtering through the leaves of an elm tree growing outside their house. "Hi, love," Riley said. "Want to hold her?" I nodded, tears rising in my throat as I reached for our daughter, who was swaddled in a soft green flannel blanket.

"Hi, baby," I said, cradling her small warm weight in my arms. Somehow both vast and impossibly tiny, she blinked up at me with deep-blue eyes. I remembered the water glinting in the distance as Riley and I unwittingly cast a love spell. I looked into Sasha's eyes, and the lake winked back, its slow magic finally made real.

LEARNING TO STAY

The first time I saw our house, I cried.

It was a hot, dry day in early July. The house, a grey-and-white bi-level built in the 1970s, looked washed out in the midday sun. The lawn around it was parched yellow by a heat wave. As I stood in the driveway, I could hear the whoosh of passing cars on the road where I now owned a quarter of a house.

Not just any house.

This house.

Our house.

My house.

Fuck.

You know how sometimes, when you buy things on the internet, they don't feel real until they arrive and you're confronted with an expensive and unreturnable object you'd thought you wanted? That day, I learned this feeling applies to houses too.

It was the second summer of the COVID pandemic. Our urban-dwelling family was ready to move to a bigger house in a smaller community. I was tired of the hour-long commute between my one-bedroom condo in the city and my co-parents' compact suburban townhouse, where I had been spending half of each week since 2018, when Sasha was born.

The townhouse was crowded with Riley, Nic, and me working from home, especially on days when three-year-old Sasha's preschool was closed. Mars was trying to get pregnant with our second child. Our family needed more space, and we couldn't afford a house big enough in Vancouver. It was time to leave the place I had called home for twenty years.

The grey-and-white house was in a semi-rural community on southern Vancouver Island. Only Nic and Riley saw it in person before we put in an offer. Mars and I agreed to buy it based on photos from a real estate website. We had been searching for months, but we kept losing bidding wars to people with bigger budgets. The longer it took to find an affordable home, the more willing I was to buy a house sight unseen.

Our offer was accepted in May, but the grey-and-white house wouldn't officially be ours for nearly two months. This allowed me to treat it more as fiction than fact, the story of an imagined future I was playing along with but not yet prepared to inhabit. Reality slammed into me with the force of a speeding U-Haul that hot summer day when I saw our new house for the first time.

The realtor, a blond woman in her fifties who looked fresh despite the heat, was waiting outside the front door when we pulled into the gravel driveway. "Congratulations!" she said, as she handed over the keys. She had us pose for a photo—the happy homeowners. I plastered on a smile that didn't reach my eyes.

I trailed behind the group as I crossed the threshold into our house for the first time, closing the door behind me. I kept a mental tally of everything I didn't like as we explored its thirteen rooms: the mismatched light fixtures, the denim-coloured countertops, the brownish ring around the bathtub drain. The grey-and-white house smelled wrong, like fake floral cleaner and other people's dust.

Our last stop on the tour was the backyard, a huge rectangle of grass and dirt that used to be farmland. It was surrounded by a wooden fence meant for keeping deer out and children in. Sasha ran onto the lawn, whooping with delight at having a yard bigger than the concrete postage stamp she was used to. Nic, Riley, Mars, and our realtor explored the backyard, pointing out where we could put garden beds, a chicken coop, and a swing.

The sun hammered my head, neck, and shoulders as I walked away from the group. Turning my back on the house, I stood under a patch of shade in the farthest corner of the yard, where grass gave way to a tangle of weeds. I could feel my family's eyes on me, but they knew to give me space.

"What have I done?" I whispered to the fence, hot tears rolling down my cheeks. A raven called, hidden in the branches of a fir tree.

I was desperate for a way out, flight instincts on overdrive, mind racing through scenarios where my family moved and I kept my apartment in the city. None were realistic. There was no way I was trading a one-hour bus commute for a five-hour trip involving a car and a ferry. I didn't want my life to feel any more separate from my family's than it already did.

The raven unfurled its wings, swooping into the air above me. If only leaving were so easy.

My mother's capacity for flight lives in my bones, a precious and complicated inheritance. I sometimes joke that if I could bring only one trauma response with me to a desert island, I would always choose flight. But it's not really a joke, is it? The leavers among us know our disappearing acts take many forms. We might be sitting beside you on the couch, plotting our escape. We might be alone in the next room with the door closed. We might already be gone.

If leaving has helped you survive, how do you learn to stay?

When I started working on this essay about living with my family, I surprised myself by writing about doors: our house's navy-blue front door with textured-glass panels, the varnished plywood pocket door to an attic apartment I lived in as a child, the doorway to our kitchen, the fireproof white apartment door I shut behind me when I walked away from my marriage, the imitation-wood door of the office where I wrote most of this book.

In *The Poetics of Space*, Gaston Bachelard writes, "If one were to give an account of all the doors one has closed and opened, of all the doors one would like to re-open, one would have to tell the story of one's entire life."[1]

At first, I thought of the doors in my story only as exits or barriers, physical evidence of a habit of leaving. Then I remembered that doorways are thresholds. A threshold is a place, but it can also be the point at which something changes.

This is a story about leaving. It is also a story about learning to stay.

If we are expecting you, someone will shout, "Come in!" when you knock on our front door. You will let yourself in without knocking if you are a friend or family member, calling out a hello as you enter. As you take off your shoes, your eyes might land on the jumble of colourful children's footwear just inside the entryway. Miniature orange rain boots with fox faces on the toes sit on a low wooden shelf near the door, beside a matching blue-and-yellow pair patterned with sharks. Their soles are compact enough to cup in my palm, but it is a fleeting smallness. The twins will soon outgrow them.

You might comment appreciatively on my daughter's iridescent-rainbow unicorn sneakers—adults with an eye for the fabulous usually do. The soles pulse with white light when she runs or jumps. I cringed at the cost, but her delight was worth the price. Her more practical pink-and-navy rain boots are toppled beside the shoe rack, kicked off in a rush to go upstairs and watch cartoons. She leaves a trail of inside-out socks in her wake, preferring to go barefoot indoors. "You have hot feet," I tell her. "Just like your Momo." She and Riley both sleep with one foot sticking out of the covers, blankets pulled tight around their shoulders.

On the wall opposite the kid-sized shoe rack is a waist-high wood-and-metal one housing a more sedate palette of practical adult shoes. It holds four pairs of almost-identical sturdy black or dark-brown leather ankle boots—Blundstones, a queer wardrobe staple here in our part of the Pacific Northwest. Maybe you'll add yours to the collection when you visit.

Sometimes, I inadvertently grab the wrong pair when leaving the house. I can tell they aren't mine as soon as I put them on, the fit too roomy, the contours all wrong. There is something shockingly intimate about putting my foot into someone else's shoe. I shudder at the strangeness of it, finding relief in the familiar embrace of my own black boots.

The road to our house is lined with tall Douglas fir trees. Seven more keep watch over our backyard, where hawks and eagles fly overhead. No matter how often we sweep or vacuum, there are always dried fir needles in our entryway. One might stow away on the bottom of your sock. If it's autumn, we'll ply you with plums or apples from our fruit trees. Arms overspilling with sweetness, you'll leave our home nourished by the land.

I stood facing the fence in the corner of the yard, self-conscious about our realtor seeing me cry. I thought back to the May afternoon when she phoned to tell us our bid on the grey-and-white house was successful.

I had been holed up in Riley's bedroom catching a few hours of work before a family dinner in celebration of my birthday. Riley was downstairs with Mars and Sasha when Nic got the realtor's call. I tuned out the excited chatter drifting up from the living room, my attention focused on the book manuscript in front of me. A few minutes later, there was a knock on Riley's bedroom door.

"Yes?" I said from where I sat cross-legged on the bed, not bothering to get up.

"We got the house!" Nic said through the door.

"Cool," I said flatly.

Nic didn't say anything after that. I heard the floor creak as she went back downstairs.

I felt guilty for not being able to muster more enthusiasm about this life-changing news and for not being gracious enough to receive it from Nic through an open door. I should have been sharing in the excitement, but instead I was resigned. *This is it. It's really happening*. I stood up to stretch, trying to loosen the tightness in my arms and legs before going back to work.

"Hey, babe," Riley said a little later, coming into their room. "Are you okay?"

"Yeah," I said, gesturing at the papers in front of me. "Just concentrating."

"Great news about the house, right? We finally get to live together full-time."

"I know," I said. "I can't wait."

I wanted to sleep in the same bed as Riley every night. I was sick of missing so much of Sasha's childhood. I wanted a less bifurcated life. I was always missing someone or something: my partner, our daughter, the easy camaraderie of our big family dinners, or the pleasure I found in solitude and the freedom of moving at my own pace. I wanted a life that made room for all of this and more. Was it possible for it to exist under one roof?

Riley, Nic, Mars, and I spent years envisioning how we might live together as a family, but when I went all in, I panicked. I had already left one home behind when my marriage collapsed. Now, instead of a spouse, I was committing to several people, which somehow seemed riskier. What if it fell apart and I was left alone to start over again? I was scared of dreaming and losing it all.

The July air was warm on my skin as I stood in our backyard trying to conjure the parts of me ready to make a home with Riley, Sasha, Nic, and Mars. The loudest voice inside me shouted *RUN!* But when I listened closely, there was a quieter voice too. It said *Stay*.

I looked back at my family, now clustered around an apple tree, Riley giving Sasha a boost as she climbed into its lowest branches. I turned toward my family, swiping a palm across my cheek to wipe away the last of my tears.

If I were to recount my mother's life story as a chronology of leaving, I would tell you about the times she crossed thresholds in search of greater freedom and safety. I would tell you about her escapes from men who harmed her. I would tell you that every time she crossed a threshold in search of greater freedom and safety, she was escaping a man.

The home where my mother grew up was not a safe place for women or children. In 1967, when she was twenty, she escaped her father's house by marrying a man who didn't cook or clean, chose all of her clothes for her, and made her sell her car because "Girls don't drive." Being his wife was preferable to living with her father.

My mother, who worked as a secretary at an insurance company, turned her paycheques over to her husband, who gave her an allowance. What he did not give her in three years of marriage was an orgasm. In 1970, when she was twenty-three, she left her husband for the sexy doctor who showed her what she had been missing. Her relationship with the doctor didn't last, but it helped her get free.

In 1979, my thirty-two-year-old mother fled my abusive father. She was eight months pregnant. She drove two thousand kilometres with my bassinet in the back seat to make sure her daughter was born into safety.

In 1986, my thirty-nine-year-old mother and I moved from Hamilton to Thunder Bay. We made the fourteen-hundred-kilometre trip by train. I was a seven-year-old girl boiling with rage at her mother for making me leave behind my family, my friends, and the place I knew as home.

I would especially miss my grandma, who spoke with a soft Scottish burr, smelled like Noxzema, and let me have Corn Pops for breakfast. My grandpa built me a playhouse in their backyard, but alcoholism made him moody. My grandparents lived in Hamilton, in the same house where my mother grew up. She had reconciled with them—or was desperate enough for an occasional night off to let me have sleepovers there. My grandparents doted on me, the only girl in a generation of boy cousins.

Was it a coincidence that we moved to Thunder Bay just after my seventh birthday, or was my mother afraid I had reached an age that made me a target? What drove her to put so much distance between my grandfather and me? My seven-year-old daughter sleeps in the next room as I write. When I consider the lengths I would go to protect her, I unsheath the blade I keep in my spine.

My mother showed me that sometimes you have to leave everything behind to protect the person you love. By leaving, she taught me we were worthy of saving. She taught me not to overvalue my capacity for endurance. She taught me the fiercest kind of loyalty at the same time as teaching me that commitment was dangerous. Our relationship was safe; relying on anyone else was too risky. Love hard, but always have an escape plan.

Our kitchen pulls visitors toward it like a magnet. A big east-facing room with warm wood tones, it is our home's liveliest and most busy space. It has two entrances. You will probably come through the one at the top of the stairs leading from our front door. Our kitchen's doorless doorway is a threshold beckoning you to cross it.

The window above our kitchen sink has a view of the backyard. We fling it open to shout back and forth with whoever is outside: "Dinner's ready!" or "Do you need me to bring out the ketchup?" Children's treasures wash up like flotsam on the mottled-grey Formica island: a metallic turquoise kazoo, a small black LEGO piece shaped like the bucket of an excavator, a dented light-blue tin containing a collection of twenty-five chestnuts, four different-sized grey pebbles tucked under the lip of the fruit bowl.

The kids' playroom opens onto the kitchen. Their games spill over into the spaces where we cook and eat. I cook dinner or wash dishes while dodging Corin and Alder racing around the room with fat pink stuffed pig-unicorns in doll strollers, or I pretend to be felled by Sasha, who is into snakes this week and is slithering around my ankles like a hungry anaconda. The kids might be shy with you at first but will eventually invite you into their games. Their favourite adults are the ones who aren't too self-conscious to act like an animal or laugh at a fart.

Our family eats dinner together in the kitchen every night. We sit at a long wooden table handed down by Riley's great-aunt, chatting about our days as we pass dishes back and forth and fail to convince the twins not to throw food on the floor. When we have friends or family over, there might be ten of us around the table. We will put out an extra place setting for you and bring up more chairs from storage. There is always room for someone else to join us.

The kitchen feels like the heart of our home.

It is also the room I am most likely to want to escape from.

My friend Leila texts me a meme while we are chatting about the ups and downs of living with others. It is a black line drawing of two people-shaped figures standing side by side. The figure on the left is mostly white inside with red scribbles up to its ankles. The text under it reads, "My anger level usually." The figure on the right is completely filled in with red scribbles. The black text below it reads, "My anger level when someone is in the kitchen with me." "I feel so seen," I reply, adding a crying-with-laughter emoji.

"I am choosing interdependence," I remind myself through gritted teeth on mornings when the kitchen feels too crowded, the kids too loud, the atmosphere too thick with other people's needs. I zigzag across the room, trying to find a clear path to the toaster. When I get there, I discover someone else is using it. My stomach growls as I shift impatiently from foot to foot with two slices of frozen multigrain bread in my hand.

My body fills with angry red scribbles.

I scan the room, searching for the clearest path to an exit.

It was early evening, the July sun still hanging high over the horizon. Riley, Sasha, and I had just arrived for a three-night stay at a tiny vacation rental tucked on a forested road surrounded by farmers' fields. Our temporary home had three rooms: a kitchen, a bathroom, and a bedroom Riley and I would share with Sasha. Nic and Mars were staying at the grey-and-white house, sleeping on air mattresses because all of our furniture was still on the mainland.

A murk of feelings clouded the air between Riley and me. The wisp of hopefulness I'd clutched in the backyard earlier had been blown away by a storm of anxieties. Riley and I kept our attention focused on Sasha, projecting a facade of calm as we fed her a dinner of boxed macaroni and cheese, read her bedtime stories, and tucked her into the borrowed playpen beside our bed with her blankie and favourite stuffed dog.

Once Sasha was asleep, Riley and I sat at the kitchen table on hard wooden chairs. I shivered, my black-and-white-striped cotton tank top inadequate protection against our ground-level suite's chilly air. Riley tried reaching for my hand, but I pulled away. The idea of softening into their touch felt too vulnerable. I was in survival mode, my icy flesh a suit of armour.

"I've decided that I can't move here," I said, my voice clipped. "I'm going to figure out a way to keep my apartment in the city."

"That doesn't make sense," Riley said, shaking their head. "I know the house isn't everything we dreamed of, but I think it can work for us."

"I thought so too, until I saw it in person. This is all your fault. I should never have believed you and Nic when you told me this was the one," I hissed.

Riley's mouth crumpled with hurt.

I knew I was being unfair. Buying the house was my decision too, but I was so caught up in my own feelings that I couldn't find it in me to apologize.

"Let's talk about this tomorrow," said Riley. "I'm going to bed." They walked the short distance to the bedroom, shoulders slumped as if to protect their heart.

I heard Riley crying through the bedroom door as I sat at the table researching flights and ferries to the mainland. A framed map of Vancouver Island hung on the wall. My eyes kept straying to the expanse of ocean between me and the city I still thought of as home. The distance between us felt almost as impassable as the gulf between Riley and me.

It can't always be easy to love a runner.

After a decade together, Riley has become adept at noticing my exit strategies. Earlier in our relationship, this sometimes looked like me physically leaving the building. In moments of acute stress, like when I saw the grey-and-white house for the first time, it can take the form of elaborately plotted escape plans. These days, I'm more likely to leave the room or to stay physically present while some part of me retreats to an emotional hideout.

In these moments, Riley might say, "Don't leave." It's a gentle plea. I receive their words as an invitation, not a demand, which makes me more likely to listen. I stay because I have the freedom to leave if I must, and because I feel safe.

My love for Riley still surprises me for how easy it feels. "Easy" doesn't mean perfect or faking it or hiding our messiest parts. It doesn't mean boring or trading our wildness for security. It means we're safe enough to show each other our whole selves and brave enough to examine and tend to our wounds. Healing isn't so much a destination as a process we engage in together. Now, when I notice myself eyeing the exits or unhooking from my body, I'm better at slowing down and discerning what will serve the relationship. I still leave sometimes, but I do it on purpose, and I know how to come back.

I wasn't ready to become a parent when Riley and I first started dating. I needed to feel more secure and at home in myself before I could become a refuge for Sasha, Alder, and Corin. My love for my children is a root system that keeps me tethered to them. I stay because I want them to know how it feels to be adored by a safe adult they can rely on. I stay for the joy, pleasure, and wonder of growing with them. I stay because being separated from my children for too long would shatter my heart.

For the first three years of Sasha's life, I kept an apartment where I lived half the time. I wasn't ready to give it up. It was the home I had created for myself after the upheaval of my mother's death and my divorce. I needed to know I had a secure base to return to, so I alternated between homes. In one, I relished the freedom and safety of my own private hideaway. In the other, I experienced belonging, interdependence, and the opportunity to practise building relationships of mutual commitment and care.

Today, I live full-time in the grey-and-white house. Sharing a home with six people can feel crowded. We are all under the microscope of intimacy. My family sees more of me than anyone else does. They know when I'm tired, stressed, cranky, irritated, sick, sad, or mad. They know when I'm anxious or activated. They know when I'm happy. Our home has private spaces, but we can't hide from each other for long. I used to want to run from this. Now, I understand how being seen is a necessary precondition of being known. I can show my whole self here and trust that I belong, which makes it feel like home.

I am the sole adult in our family with a room of my own. Having an office with a door I can close was a condition of agreeing to dwell with so many others. I spend a lot of time swimming in our home's shared waters. This small, square room is my life raft in a sea of interdependence.

When I tour visitors through our house, they are more likely to walk into our bathroom or the bedroom I share with Riley than into my office. It's like an invisible force field keeps people out. Does coming in here feel like you're riffling through my underwear drawer? Riley tells me they have learned not to talk to me if I'm working at my desk with the door open. "You growl at me if I interrupt you!" they say with a laugh. I accept this truth about myself with a rueful grin.

I am harder to live with if I can't close a door between me and my family at least once a day. Specifically, a white, six-panel wood-grain door with a faux brass knob and a hollow core, the kind you can buy for a hundred dollars at Home Depot. Sound travels through it, a permeable membrane. Sometimes, I hear a crying child call my name from down the hall. "ZeeZee! ZeeZee!" they wail. Most of the time, I go to them. Sasha occasionally slides notes and drawings under my door. When she does this, I feel loved and also guilty. I am not a mother, but that doesn't stop me from feeling like a bad one.

Yet my children also treat my office as a trove of useful art supplies—a hole punch, a purple metal ruler, glitter washi tape, metallic Sharpies, fine-tipped coloured pens. Alder and Corin take rides on my raspberry-coloured desk chair, spinning in circles until they're so dizzy they wobble like drunken sailors. They ask me to draw pictures for them on scrap paper. "A red horse! A banana! A blue bike!" They're fascinated by my knick-knacks, especially a pair of magenta and navy blue articulated plastic slugs whom they've dubbed Bonnie and Merlin.

When I need to close the door and go back to work, I tell my children that I am writing a book about our family. If they ever read it, I hope they will see it as the love letter it is.

It is not lost on me that I usually sit in solitude behind a closed door to write about being with others. But even then, I am not alone. If you look at the wall beside my desk, you will see a small altar with photographs of my mother, my grandmother, and my great-grandmother holding me as a baby or young child. The centrepiece is a large black-and-white photo of me as a toddler sitting on my mother's lap. I smile at the camera, head tilted toward a bouquet of snapdragons on a nearby table. My mother presses her lips to my hair, breathing me in.

My vision adjusted to the early morning light streaming through the slats of the white wooden blinds. It was just after sunrise. Riley slept beside me with one foot sticking out from under the navy polka-dot duvet. Sasha rustled in her playpen. Her stirrings told me she would be awake soon, but there were still a few minutes before she would call out for Riley and me.

I yawned, rubbing grit from my eyes. My neck was stiff from our rental's too-fluffy pillows. It had taken me hours to fall asleep last night after Riley went to bed. I sat in the kitchen until midnight writing in my journal, too wired to rest. I wasn't sure whether to reread what I wrote. Did I want to revisit the version of me who'd spewed out five pages of hurt, anger, and reasons to leave? I was ashamed of how I had treated Riley. It wasn't fair to blame them for my decision to buy the grey-and-white house.

I swallowed, trying to loosen the apology stuck in my throat. How could I find the words to explain the parts shouting *RUN*? It was like living with an animal, except the animal was me. I rolled over, wrapping my arm around Riley's waist. They nestled into me, their body warm against my chest, belly, and thighs. "I'm sorry," I whispered. "I'm so sorry."

"I know," Riley mumbled, still half asleep. They laced their fingers through mine like a promise not to let me go.

I haven't learned to stay. I'm learning. My commitment to building a family with Riley, Mars, Nic, Sasha, Alder, and Corin isn't a choice I made once. It's a threshold I cross again and again. Every time I come home to the grey-and-white house, I renew my promise.

Overnight transformation narratives might be seductive, but they're rarely the whole story. I've been with Riley for ten years. We've been co-parenting with Mars and Nic for seven, since Sasha was born. Her birth knitted us into a family because of how intensely we came to depend on each other, and because she was the centre of our solar system until our universe expanded to include Alder and Corin three years later. Her younger siblings were born soon after we moved into the grey-and-white house. It is the only home they have ever known.

In *The Breaks*, Julietta Singh writes of how "relationships develop within and against the architectural shapes that house us. Architecture anticipates ways of living in the spaces we rent or buy, presumes conventions of living that are literally built into the structures we dwell in."[2] Many North American homes are designed for a nuclear family. The grey-and-white house isn't all that different. We chose it because we could envision ways of inhabiting its private and shared spaces that would work for our sprawling queer family. We are together enough, and apart enough, to make our commitments to each other feel more possible. One reason I love our bustling kitchen is that there is somewhere else for me to go when I am overwhelmed by the din.

Singh dwells alongside and co-parents with Nathan Snaza, her ex-spouse turned chosen family. They use the notion of "queer architectures" to articulate how, "by pure necessity or needful desire, some of us make a craft of ... subverting architectural presumptions by living in and against them otherwise."[3] As a married couple, they inhabited a small three-bedroom house whose layout Singh describes as a "hetero endgame."[4] As queer co-parents, they share a duplex with their daughter where they coexist "in the felt rhythms of [their] lives unfolding."[5]

How we make family is another form of queer architecture. It took years for me to trust Riley, Nic, and Mars enough to make a home together, even after our daughter was born. My internal landscape has become more capacious since moving into the grey-and-white house. While the constant proximity of others sometimes chafes, I wouldn't choose to live otherwise. There is too much pleasure to be gained from waking up to my children's small, bright faces and falling asleep beside

Riley's beloved shape every night. May our love for each other be a shelter inside this sturdy home we have made, are making, will keep making as our lives unfold.

Our backyard looks more alive now than it did on that hot July day four years ago. In summer, the raised garden beds in the northeast corner are a riot of cherry tomato plants, kale, arugula, and the odd squash. We have two apple trees and a plum tree that start blooming in spring and bear fruit in autumn. We'll have an abundant harvest this year. The lawn, more green than yellow, is dotted with clusters of dandelions the same colour as Corin and Alder's matching toy dump trucks.

Our house sits on a half-acre, the yard a giant rectangle bordered by a wooden fence with tall purple and fuchsia rhododendrons on one side. On the other, our next-door neighbours' blackberry and rose bushes trail over our fence, teasing us with their wild, spiky beauty. In August, our children beg us to boost them up high enough to pick sun-warmed berries, sweet juices staining their hands and faces purple.

Your body might soften in relief when you realize your children can roam freely here, giving you a moment's respite to chat, eat, or sip a cool drink. Kids love the trampoline, the hand-me-down pink plastic playhouse, the climbing net, and the swing. There's lots of space to run, bike, or kick a ball around. We have a hammock for you to lounge in, sturdy green patio chairs with and without arms so you can sit comfortably, and blankets for napping on the grass.

Several times a year, we host big barbecues and other gatherings in our backyard. I love seeing it filled with friends and friends of friends and strangers from the local queer Facebook group. When I left Vancouver, I brought with me the skills I had gained from two decades of community building. I continue tending my relational web in the city while weaving a new one here. Moving to an island in my forties has made me aggressively earnest about making friends. I'm proud that our family is known for our care and generosity as hosts.

I tell Riley I want to put my hands in the dirt, but I hardly ever follow through. Riley and Nic do most of the yardwork, while Mars pitches in on gardening. Turns out I'm better at growing friendships than food or flowers. I'm not used to having a backyard, even after four years of living here. As a kid, I grew up always moving from apartment to apartment, poverty starving my mother's ability to keep us rooted in one place. I know how to make an unfamiliar space feel like home, but I'm still learning how to build a long-term relationship with the land.

When I first arrived at the grey-and-white-house, I salted the earth with my tears. Now, when I feel the sun-warmed grass and dirt of our yard under my bare feet, it reminds me that I can keep growing here, and I will.

I put the loaf of olive bread from the farmers' market down on the kitchen counter. It was going to be delicious served with cheese. My stomach rumbled in anticipation of second breakfast. Stress stole my appetite yesterday. I took my hunger as a positive sign. All of my doubts about the grey-and-white house hadn't dissipated overnight, but the voice shouting *RUN!* was quieter this morning. Through the kitchen window, I saw leggy Douglas firs, their green branches bright against the dried-out lawn. The linoleum was cool under my bare feet.

I had come home to my body. The space around me looked different without panic fogging my vision.

I heard Sasha giggling as she played hide-and-seek in empty closets. She was downstairs with Riley, Nic, and Mars, who were taking measurements and discussing ways to make the house's various spaces work for us. I had already claimed a small upstairs room as my office. It was across the hall from the bedroom I would share with Riley. I liked that our bed would have a view of trees and open skies.

I followed the voices downstairs, where I found Riley, Nic, and Mars in the half kitchen adjoining what would become our guest room. "We were just talking about how we could use this closet as a pantry," said Nic, gesturing behind her.

"Yeah, and we can take the doors off to make it easier to access," said Mars.

I nodded, taking Riley's hand as I caught up on what I had missed.

"Sounds like a great idea," I said, and meant it. The downstairs kitchen had a back door that opened onto the yard. "Hey, does anyone want to go outside with me? I'm curious what the backyard is like when we're not baking in the afternoon sun."

"I do!" said Sasha, popping out of the closet like a jack-in-the-box.

"You surprised me," I said, laughing. Her mischievous grin reminded me of Riley's.

Sasha led us outside in a tiny parade. She made a beeline for the apple tree. "I want to climb it again!" she shouted.

"Okay," said Riley, cupping their hands together to give her a boost onto one of the tree's lower branches.

Sasha's chubby toddler legs dangled in the air as she gazed up at the canopy of leaves. "Look," she said, pointing at one of the tree's upper branches. "Apples." Riley, Nic, Mars, and I followed her finger to where a cluster of tiny green apples was growing. The tree was blanketed with them. They weren't yet ready to eat, but it seemed as if we would have a plentiful fall harvest.

A promise of a sweeter future, if we were patient enough to stick around and help it grow.

BEST INTERESTS OF THE CHILD

I, Zena Catherine Sharman [full name], **writer** [occupation], **of** ███ ████████████████████ [address of party, city, province].

SWEAR OR AFFIRM THAT:

I know or believe the following facts to be true. If these facts are based on information from others, I believe that information to be true.

Before you can complete the affidavit, you must complete the following background checks referenced in the form:

- *a Ministry of Children and Family Development record check*
- *a protection order record check from the Protection Order Registry, and*
- *a criminal record check*

To get a criminal record check, ask at the police station or RCMP detachment in your community.

We talk through a hole in a thick pane of bulletproof glass. I am on the side reserved for people who need things or people who are in trouble. I am here because I need something, but I already feel like I am in trouble. The glass is there to protect her from us.

I wear a black raincoat and a leopard-print scarf to ward off the November chill. The woman on the other side of the glass wears a soft turquoise sweater, her dyed-blond hair styled in a neat bob. She looks like someone I would run into at the garden centre or grocery store. In a city this small, I probably have.

"How old are the children?" she asks, shuffling through my criminal record check forms.

"A six-year-old and two-year-old twins," I say. I stop myself from fidgeting with my pen, trying to project an air of relaxed inculpability. I put on my most palatable face, belatedly wondering if wearing red lipstick was the wrong choice for this errand.

She looks up from my paperwork like she suddenly sees all of me. "Good for you," she says. The emphasis she puts on the first word tells me I have been deemed good. Her gust of warmth shifts the atmosphere between us. For me, it is a rupture; for her, a bridge. She treats me like I am a heroic older woman rescuing an irresponsible family member's children from foster care. I am being handed a Citizen of the Year trophy I neither want nor deserve.

She has twin sons, she tells me, reminiscing about when they were small. She smiles as she says one of them grew up to become a police officer. I resist the urge to say, "My condolences."

"Are your twins boys or girls?" she asks.

I have learned to anticipate this question—adults are obsessed with categorizing children. They sometimes become hostile when I refuse to give them a satisfying answer. I weigh my options: lie to keep this interaction smooth, or tell the truth because I'm at the police station getting paperwork that will eventually be reviewed by a judge. My fear of being punished for lying outweighs my desire to keep things easy between us.

"We're doing gender-open parenting, so we're going to wait until the twins are old enough to tell us who they are," I say, my voice rising a little with every word. "It's different but it works for us," I say, shrugging. I become a wide-eyed, floppy-earned bunny, intent on distracting her with how unthreatening I am so she doesn't go for my throat.

The way her eyes narrow when she hears the words *gender-open parenting* makes it clear that telling the truth was the wrong choice.

The glass between us frosts over. She has gone from relaxed and friendly to coolly efficient. She stops chatting about the highs and lows of raising twins and becomes intently focused on making photocopies of my driver's licence and passport.

She doesn't say it out loud but I can tell she is thinking it: *groomer*. I wonder if she went to the Save the Children–themed anti-trans rally organized recently in town. No longer good in her eyes, I am a threat and a pervert, trying to secure access to children I don't deserve to care for. She would save them from me if she could.

I wonder if I have blown my chance at getting what I need from her. My stomach twists. I stand like a supplicant on my side of the glass, hoping the barrier between us will keep her hate from seeping under my skin.

In 1975, Minnie Bruce Pratt left her husband to live openly as a lesbian. She had two young sons. When she asserted her sexual independence, "the world looked at me and saw an unfit mother," Pratt wrote in 1993. "Suddenly, my husband had legal grounds to take my children away from me and never let me see them again."[1] As an out queer woman, she was subject to felony charges under North Carolina's "crime against nature" statutes.[2] Her lawyer told her, "You don't have a dog's chance in court."[3] Pratt lost custody of her sons, Ben and Ransom, to her ex-husband. Her divorce settlement forbade her from having her children in her home if she lived with another person, and she could only take them out of their home state if they were going to visit her mother. Pratt used to drive fourteen hours each way on three-day weekends to see them.

Pratt's story is notable to me because she is one of my femme literary heroes, and because it exemplifies the consequences of an era when same-sex sexuality was construed as "antithetical to parenting."[4] Historians and legal scholars have demonstrated how, between the 1960s and 1990s, queer parents in the US and Canada frequently lost custody of their children, if they were allowed to see them at all. As more LGBTQ+ people began coming out of the closet and leaving heterosexual marriages, they often found themselves in the impossible position of choosing between living authentically and maintaining relationships with their children.

The US legal regime "centred on the assumption that same-sex sexuality was inherently dangerous to children."[5] It was feared that queer parents would pass on their deviant desires to their offspring and that their children would face stigma and psychological damage. Queer people—especially gay men—were stereotyped as pedophiles. One judge said he would "not permit 'children to be placed in a home where the felony of sodomy is committed at least twice a week.'"[6] Some parents who were allowed to retain custody or visitation rights were barred from seeing their children in the presence of their same-sex partners and prohibited from participating in queer community activism or social events. Others were required to sign affidavits consenting to regular psychiatric examinations testifying to having repudiated their sexual orientation.[7]

In Canada, the queer parents who won custody of their children did so by "leaning into a politics of respectability" and discretion.[8] Parents who were open, proud activists or involved in the queer community were more likely to lose child custody or access. The first reported Canadian case in which a lesbian mother was awarded custody of her child was *K v K* (Alberta, 1975). Halnya Freeland, the feminist lawyer who acted on Mrs. K's behalf, later wrote that the judge commented favourably in his decision on how discreet the mother was about her lesbianism. Freeland added that she believed the mother would have lost custody "had the father not been found completely incapable of caring for the child."[9] A year earlier, in *Case v Case*, a lesbian mother in Saskatchewan lost custody of her two children because the judge ruled that her gay rights activism would be harmful to them. The line between "good" and "bad" lesbian mothers hinged in part on acting straight, and on a promise to raise their children to be heterosexual.[10]

Pratt loved her children fiercely and refused the idea that lesbianism made her a bad mother. Her sons, then aged ten and eleven, helped her print and assemble her first chapbook, *The Sound of One Fork* (1981).[11] They used equipment owned by Lollipop Power, a North Carolina–based publisher of feminist children's books with titles like *Grownups Cry Too* and *I Like You to Make Jokes with Me, but I Don't Want You to Touch Me*. Eight years later, Firebrand Books published *Crime Against Nature*, Pratt's award-winning poetry collection about her experiences as a lesbian mother deemed unfit to parent. In the titular poem, she wrote, "I didn't write this story until now when [my sons] are too old for either law or father to seize or prevent [them] from hearing my words."[12] Sodomy was still illegal in half of US states when *Crime Against Nature* was published.[13] Although ruled unconstitutional in 2003, these laws are still in effect in twelve states, including North Carolina.[14]

In her afterword to the 2013 Sinister Wisdom edition of *Crime Against Nature*, Pratt wrote, "When my children were taken from me, I said, 'I have nothing left to lose.' I meant that the system of ownership and bigotry had almost killed me with grief. If I was not to die, then I was going to have to live—to fight to change everything."[15] In a 2021 interview, Pratt encouraged young people to be brave. "There's a place for you," she says. "It's wonderful to be able to look back and say you have led the life that you wanted to lead."[16] She died in 2023 with her family at her side.

PARAGRAPH 1

I am making this affidavit in support of an application under the Family Law Act to become a guardian of the following child(ren):

CHILD'S FULL NAME	CHILD'S DATE OF BIRTH [MM/DD/YYYY]	NAME(S) OF CHILD'S CURRENT GUARDIAN(S)	NAME(S) OF CHILD'S PARENT(S) WHO ARE NOT CURRENT GUARDIAN(S)
████████	████████	████████	Zena Sharman
████████	████████	████████	Zena Sharman
████████	████████	████████	Zena Sharman

The nature and length of my relationship with the child(ren) referred to in paragraph 1 of this affidavit is as follows:

1) The nature and length of my relationship with the child(ren) referred to in paragraph 1 of this affidavit began ten years ago, when I fell in love with someone who was trying to have a baby with two other people.

2) The nature and length of my relationship with the child(ren) referred to in paragraph 1 of this affidavit began eight years ago in a suburban

bedroom, where I inseminated Riley with the sperm that helped make our daughter. It was the summer solstice. Riley was ovulating. Instead of going to a concert in the city, we stayed home to make a baby. We had already tried enough times that the act of creation felt mundane. The magic came several weeks later, when we found out it worked.

3) The nature and length of my relationship with the child(ren) referred to in paragraph 1 of this affidavit began seven years ago when my co-parents Nic and Mars and I watched Riley give birth to our daughter, Sasha. I didn't insist on holding her that night because I feared I hadn't earned the right to call myself a parent.

4) The nature and length of my relationship with the child(ren) referred to in paragraph 1 of this affidavit began seven years ago when I held Sasha for the first time. She was eighteen hours old. In a photograph from that day, I hold her small sleeping body close to my chest. I am smiling so widely my gums are showing.

5) The nature and length of my relationship with the child(ren) in paragraph 1 of this affidavit began seven years ago when I started spending half of each week in the suburbs with my partner, my co-parents, and our daughter. My pink unicorn pyjamas lived there full-time.

6) The nature and length of my relationship with the child(ren) in paragraph 1 of this affidavit began four years ago when I sold my apartment and moved to a house on an island with my family. We knew Mars was pregnant, but several more months would pass before we found out we were having twins.

7) The nature and length of my relationship with the children referred to in paragraph 1 of this affidavit began three years ago, when Mars gave

birth to the twins by C-section. The hospital only allowed birthing people to have one support person with them in the operating suite and on the maternity ward. Riley went to the hospital with Mars while Nic and I stayed home. I washed the kitchen floor while waiting anxiously for updates. Our midwife convinced the labour and delivery ward to grant our family a temporary exception to the one-support-person policy once the twins were safely out. We were given two hours. This time, I held our babies right away.

8) The nature and length of my relationship with the children referred to in paragraph 1 of this affidavit began two years ago, on January 2, 2024, when a judge appointed me guardian of my three children. I received the news by email a day later.

Select whichever option is correct.
☑ **I am not** a parent, step-parent or guardian of any children except that child/those children referred to in paragraph 1 of this affidavit.
☑ **I am** the parent, step-parent or guardian of the following child(ren) who is/are not referred to in paragraph 1 of this affidavit.

My children's birth certificates are printed on small rectangular sheets of polymer watermarked with blue and brown maple leaves. They list each child's name, date, and place of birth, as well as the names and birthplaces of their parents. My name isn't on any of them. We aren't related by blood, marriage, surrogacy, or adoption. Yet I was part of my daughter's conception and have cared for all three children since birth. They have never asked to see paperwork proving the legitimacy of our relationship.

Queer kinship has a more capacious relational imagination than the state. In the province where I live, it is possible—thanks to queer and polyamorous people's legal advocacy—to list more than two parents on a birth certificate. When our daughter was born, you could name up to three parents as long as they were tied to the child by marriage, adoption, or shared biogenetic materials like eggs or sperm. This ruled out my co-parent Nic and me. After consulting with a lawyer, we chose to put Riley and Mars's names on our daughter's birth certificate, though we understood that even this was stretching the bounds of what was legally allowable at the time.

In 2021, a British Columbia Supreme Court judge ruled in favour of a polyamorous triad's request to register their two-and-a-half-year-old child's unrelated other mother as his third parent.[17] While this precedent was in place by the time the twins were born, we again opted to name only Mars and Riley as parents on our children's birth certificates. Just because it is possible to designate multiple parents doesn't mean it's easy. We didn't want to become another legal test case and were reluctant to spend thousands of dollars in legal fees contorting our family into a shape legible to the judicial system. This left Nic and me with tenuous legal status as our children's parents. It was a risk we were willing to take.

Our family sat comfortably around the margins of the law until our daughter started school. Until then, the durability and legitimacy of our bonds had not been tested by death, health crises, breakups, or homophobic relatives. Our whiteness, non-disabledness, and class privilege protected us from the scrutiny of the family policing system. The only social worker in our house was Mars, who wasn't going to report us to the Ministry of Children and Family Development for being weird and queer.

Enrolling Sasha in kindergarten forced our hand, as we soon realized only Riley and Mars would be officially recognized as our daughter's parents at school. We didn't want to chance having two parents unable to act on her behalf—it could be dangerous in an emergency and would limit our ability to act as her advocates with teachers and administrators. This prompted Nic and I to pursue guardianship of Sasha and her younger siblings. The alternative, step-parent adoption, seemed to us like a more legally complex, expensive, and invasive process.

"Does it matter to you that you still won't be your kids' legal parents if you become their guardians?" asked the queer family lawyer who helped us with the process.

"No," said Nic.

I nodded in agreement. "We know we're their parents," I said.

My date of birth is: XX-XX-1979

In 1979, three feminist collectives published guides to self-insemination: *Lesbian Health Matters!*, *Woman Controlled Conception*, and *Artificial Insemination: An Alternative Conception for the Lesbian and Gay Community*.[18] Until the 1980s, when the fertility industry realized single women were an untapped market, lesbians and single women faced systematic barriers to physician-assisted donor insemination. "Locked out of institutional routes to pregnancy by physician gatekeeping and hoping to avoid sex with men," writes Sarah Matthiesen in *Reproduction Reconceived*, "lesbians in the women's health self-help movement became experts in what they called 'alternative fertilization.'"[19]

While by the mid-1970s, two feminist health clinics in the US had begun offering artificial insemination services in partnership with sperm banks, most women procured sperm through friends, relatives, or donor networks operated by feminist health activists and gay male donors. *Artificial Insemination* was co-written by Jill, the pseudonym for a lesbian who had been self-inseminating for several months, and Jack, the pseudonym for a gay man who had been a donor for other lesbians. Jack was Jill's liaison—the intermediary between her and her anonymous sperm donor(s), a role sometimes called a "sperm runner."[20] Some donees and donors chose complete anonymity as further protection against future custody claims. One East Coast gay commune hosted a party where men ejaculated into clean jars, mixed together the results, and gave them to women seeking to become pregnant, bringing new meaning to the term "party favours."[21]

These efforts to reclaim community control of conception occurred during an era when feminists and gay liberationists called for the abolition of the nuclear family, promoted collective child-rearing, and imagined alternative means of reproduction. In her 1970 book, *The Dialectic of Sex*, Shulamith Firestone envisioned a world in which women were freed "from the tyranny of their reproductive biology" and where child-bearing and child-rearing were diffused "to the society as a whole, men as well as women."[22] The 1971 London Gay Liberation Front manifesto advocated for the formation of "gay communes" in which "the development of children [would become] the shared responsibility of a larger group of people who live together."[23]

Queer people put these political commitments into practice through experiments in collective child-rearing. There was a toddler whose cadre of lesbian and gay caregivers called themselves Robin's Parents Association, a seven-year-old with five parents who named themselves Myrah's Mothers, and a lesbian collective house who had another person's child living with them one night a week.[24]

Lesbians and gay men put "self-help tactics to new use" by forming grassroots networks of donors and donees in various US and Canadian cities.[25] More experienced lesbians shared their knowledge with others through written guides, workshops, and hands-on support. A San Francisco woman named Lily said she was inseminating as many as ten women a month by 1980.[26] However, the practice of self-insemination came under greater scrutiny in the early 1980s due to sensationalistic media coverage and an increasingly conservative political climate targeting gays and lesbians. The arrival of the AIDS crisis made it impossible to sustain the informal donor insemination networks that had begun in the 1970s.

The reproductive knowledge, skills, and practices contained in guides like *Lesbian Health Matters!*, *Woman Controlled Conception*, and *Artificial Insemination* still circulate in queer communities more than forty years later. My children were conceived through home insemination using sperm from known donors, using methods not all that different from those contained in the guides published the year I was born. When I wielded a syringe of sperm in my lover's bedroom, unseen queer elders and ancestors guided my hands.

The first time I cupped the swell of Riley's belly and felt our daughter flutter under my hand, I called her "party fish" because she didn't have a name yet. We tracked her growth with an app that compared her to fruits and vegetables: strawberry, mango, eggplant, watermelon. As she grew bigger, I marvelled at the strangeness of bumping up against the curve of her body when I fucked Riley. I laughed when my friend, a queer femme who works as a midwife, told me some of her straight clients fear they will hurt the baby by having penetrative sex during pregnancy. I sometimes forget that not everyone comes from lineages that teach us how to fit our hand into another's body, contracting and expanding together as we marvel at our lovers' capacity to receive.

When Riley was pregnant, I occasionally wondered what it would be like to carry a child but never enough to feel motivated to try. Pregnancy seemed to ask more of me than I was ready to give. For me, one of the gifts of queering reproduction is having others in my family willingly take on the gestational labour. I am grateful to Riley and Mars for being our children's first homes, and for the legacies of chosen kinship and collective care we are passing down to them.

I plan to care for the child(ren) referred to in paragraph 1 of this affidavit as follows: *Set out detailed plans for how the child(ren) is/are to be cared for.*

Our official answer to this question, the one we knew a judge would see, was intentionally brief: "All three children have been cared for by all four parties since birth. The parties live together and raise the children collectively."

In 1983, Lollipop Power, the publisher whose equipment Minnie Bruce Pratt and her sons used to assemble her poetry chapbook, published a children's book called *Lots of Mommies*. Written by Jane Severance, a lesbian preschool teacher in her early twenties, the picture book tells the story of a girl named Emily who is being raised by four women: Annie Jo, a carpenter; Vicki, a school bus driver; Shadowoman, a healer; and her mother, Jill, who is studying to become an electrician. While the women aren't overtly presented as lesbians, illustrator Jan Jones's pictures depict what I can only perceive as a collective house full of highly competent dykes. (See for yourself: As of today, you can read a digital copy of the book on the Internet Archive.)

Lots of Mommies takes place on Emily's first day of school. She proudly wears the striped overalls she helped Shadowoman sew. Shadowoman and Annie Jo walk Emily to school, each holding one of her hands. When they arrive, Emily says goodbye to her parents and joins a group of kids her age.

"I have a big brother and big sister," says a girl.

"I have a new baby," says a boy. "What do you have?" he asks Emily.

"Emily thought about her family," Severance writes. "Was there a word for what she had? She thought about the way everyone in her family took care of her. 'I have lots of mommies,' she said. Before she could explain, the other children began to laugh."[27]

Her peers tease her, calling her a liar, so Emily runs off alone to play on the jungle gym. She becomes so engrossed in pretending to drive a school bus through a snowstorm that she falls and dislocates her shoulder.

Various adults—a teacher, a neighbour, the school bus driver, another kid's parent—come to her aid. Each summons one of Emily's mothers, who flock to the schoolyard. Tools clanking, Annie Jo runs over from where she had been repairing a roof nearby. Jill parks her bike beside the "Absolutely No Bicycles Allowed" sign. Vicki drives up in her bus. Shadowoman lopes onto the playground, skirts swirling, where she uses her healing powers to rotate Emily's shoulder back into place.

The other children watch, awestruck.

> "She does have lots of mommies," a girl said.
> "And they all take care of her," a boy said.
> "I wish I could build things," said another girl looking at Annie Jo's hammer.[28]

(Author's note: "Looking at Annie Jo's hammer" could also be a way of describing my sexual orientation.)

Lots of Mommies was inspired by Severance's desire to write works for the lesbian community she was part of in Denver in the 1970s and 1980s. Her initial foray into children's literature was *When Megan Went Away* (1979), which tells the story of a girl mourning the breakup of her mother's lesbian relationship. Also published by Lollipop Power, it was the first children's book about lesbian mothers, predating Lesléa Newman's *Heather Has Two Mommies* by a decade.

In an interview, Severance recounts how she and her peers knew few older lesbians in the 1970s. "We were like children trying to raise each other."[29] The lesbian mothers in her circles struggled with poverty and trauma. "I did know some women who were raising children in collective households," Severance says, "but it was not as idyllic as the household shown in *Lots of Mommies*. It was a couple of really fucked-up women with lots of kids from previous marriages and the mommies all drank."[30]

About us:

You may choose to complete this section or leave this section blank.

We chose to leave this section blank.

In 1983, Gino Sikorski, a gay father, wrote a letter to the organizing committee of Santa Monica's Christopher Street West Parade, complaining about the charging of admission for children at the festival. "We feel that our children supply an air of wholesomeness to the onlooking homophobic individual who thinks of us as drug abusing, disco dancing, diseased individuals," Sikorski wrote.[31]

Two years later, in 1985, Bill Jones, a founding member of San Francisco Bay Area Gay Fathers, would recall how seeing gay fathers marching in the 1975 Gay Freedom Day Parade mitigated his discomfort at the "sleaziness of the overdone drag queens and pickup trucks loaded down with obscene signs, bare rear ends, and toilet bowls."[32] Jones emphasized how gay fathers and their children "make a powerful political statement ... with our numbers, our clean-cut look, and most of all, with the wonderful faces of our kids who look happy and well cared for."[33]

In his 2013 book *Radical Relations*, historian Daniel Winunwe Rivers points to how the radical gay fathers movement of the early 1970s became more assimilationist and politically centrist as older, more professionally established gay men came to predominate in gay fathers groups. Rivers notes that "later political campaigns for gay and lesbian parental rights and same-sex marriage would inherit this politics of gay familial and domestic respectability."[34]

Leaders in the movement to legalize same-sex marriage in the US deliberately selected "a disproportionate number of mothers and fathers to serve as plaintiffs in their [marriage equality] cases, to highlight the effects of the discriminatory laws on children."[35] The legalization of same-sex marriage was accomplished, at least in part, through racialized narratives of illegitimacy that positioned "LGBTQ+ parents (imagined as white) against unwed mothers experiencing poverty (imagined as straight and of colour)."[36] These campaigns deployed discourses of sameness and wholesome family values, "emphasizing commonalities between white middle-class same-sex couples and the traditional American family."[37]

Rather than protecting children *from* queer people, the legal regime became invested in protecting the children *of* some queer people, though this protection was conditional on conforming to normative ideals of white familial respectability.

About us:

You may choose to complete this section or leave this section blank.

What does it mean to choose to say nothing about yourself, or to show only the parts you think will be acceptable to those whose approval you are trying to gain?

I leave blanks in some of my stories, empty spaces meant to distract or elide.

When I tell straight people about our family, I often say, "We're two couples raising three children together." Our mononormative culture primes us to recognize and validate couples. If you squint just right, our family bears a passing resemblance to a blended family, except we all live together and no one had to break up for it to form.

This image—two couples working together as a team—is a useful shortcut that bypasses what I'd rather people not think about: who or how we fuck. When someone refers to Nic or Mars as my partners, I correct them. "I only have one partner, Riley," I say. "Nic and Mars are my co-parents."

I emphasize this distinction because I don't want people to think we are all fucking each other. The idea makes me uncomfortable, not just because it's an inaccurate way of characterizing our relationships, but because it feels like too much queer sex to associate with our family.

Queer sex—particularly the kind that happens outside of committed monogamous relationships, especially if it involves BDSM—is a risky activity to associate with children. I rewrote that sentence three times before I allowed myself to say "children." I kept wanting to qualify it—"parenting and children," "care of children"—but the truth is, those are all ways of putting something between queer sex and children.

By telling our family's story in ways that emphasize how normal we are, I'm playing into rhetorics of respectability that harm us and others. It's also a way of narrativizing our experiences that distances us from polyamorous families where the adults do have sexual and romantic relationships with each other. As a queer polyamorous person, this distancing feels both self-contradictory and like a betrayal of communities I consider myself part of.

To prevent strangers or acquaintances from imagining what goes on in our bedrooms, I grip a shred of respectability until it becomes a wedge.

I don't want to be like straight people, but I want them to like me.

I want them to think I'm safe enough to be around children. I want them to think their children will be safe with me.

I don't want them to take my children away.

In *Self-Portrait/Cutting* (1993), photographer Catherine Opie sits in front of a green baroque backdrop with her back to the camera. She is short haired and shirtless with a black tattooed armband and silver rings in her ears. There is a cutting on Opie's back, so fresh that the blood pools thickly in some places, almost dripping. The image cut into her skin is a child-like drawing of two stick figures in skirts holding hands. Behind them is a house with smoke coming out of its chimney. Above the skirted figures are the sun, partly hidden behind a cloud, and two birds. The image conveys her longing for domesticity; she drew pictures of it for a year before having it cut into her skin. "I wanted home, family, a wife, a child—I wanted all of that so badly. So I cut that on my back," Opie said in 2023.[38]

A year later, Opie made *Self-Portrait/Pervert* (1994). In this arrestingly beautiful image, she faces the camera, head completely covered by a black-leather hood. Twenty-three eighteen-gauge needles pierce each of Opie's arms in evenly spaced rows. The word *Pervert* is cut into her chest in elegant script, the decorative filigree incising the skin above each breast, mimicking the pattern on the black-and-gold fabric behind her. Her skin flushes red under the cutting. She has called the process of making this photograph an endurance test. Opie intended it to "push the whole realm of beauty and elegance, but also to make people scared out of their wits."[39] *Self-Portrait/Pervert* was a "direct response to the gay and lesbian community beginning to create this rhetoric of being normal. And that really bothered me, because what did that make everyone else?"[40]

Opie made *Self-Portrait/Nursing* in 2004. It depicts her, now in her forties, cradling her one-year-old son, Oliver. Opie's sturdy hands and forearms are tanned; her son's skin looks milky against his mother's. They gaze intently at each other as he nurses. The scar from Opie's "Pervert" cutting is still visible on her chest, though it has long since healed. Maggie Nelson calls the ghosted scar "a rebus of sodomitical maternity."[41] Opie's body looks softer than it did a decade earlier, her haircut a little shaggier. *Self-Portrait/Nursing* completes a trilogy that began with *Self-Portrait/Cutting*. When Opie made *Self-Portrait/Nursing*, she had realized her long-held dream of having a home, a wife, and a child. She intended this photograph to expand ideas about her body and identity. Yet, she says, "*Pervert* is still there as a scar. That's a permanent scar, and it was made to be permanent."[42]

In an essay on Opie's work, her friend Dorothy Allison, whom she came of age with in San Francisco's Leatherdyke community in the 1980s, wrote of how *Self-Portrait/Nursing* startled her every time she saw it. "It's a Madonna-and-child image with an aging, naked, dyke mama nursing a beautiful almost-toddler," Allison wrote. "I look at the light scratches above her breasts, the ones that spell out 'pervert.' For a moment, I am ashamed."[43] Allison's shame was that of self-recognition: "I could look like that, be that image, fleshy as the women pushing strollers around the Wal-Mart and casually exposing my son to the contempt of strangers."[44]

Like Opie, Allison was a lesbian mother whose art centred her communities—survivors, poor people, femmes, women who hungered for sex that transgressed norms. She spoke of the pressures she felt to be an ideal mother. "What I always thought was, if I screw up [at being a mother], nobody else will be able to have children," Allison said in a 2015 interview. "I can't fuck this up for all those other baby lesbians who want to make babies."[45]

Like me, Allison saw herself in Opie's self-portraiture. She stopped, looked again at *Self-Portrait/Nursing*, and "push[ed] away the shame. 'What would it be like,' Allison asked, 'if we could all show our secret selves this frankly?'"[46]

We believe the consent order about guardianship for the child(ren) is in their best interests because:

We understood we were being tested when we wrote our answer to this question, though we weren't sure by whose standards we were being graded:

> We believe the consent order about guardianship for the children is in their best interests because all three children have been cared for by all four parties since birth. We live together and raise the children collectively, and have created a loving, stable, supportive home environment for them. All four parties are in agreement on the benefits of formalizing Nic and Zena's parental roles and responsibilities as caregivers and decision makers for Corin, Alder, and Sasha through guardianship.

We hoped this paragraph would say enough to convince a judge to let Nic and me become our children's legal guardians, without saying so much that we would be compelled to appear in court to explain our family or justify why we were fit to care for our children. The words *loving*, *stable*, and *supportive* are accurate descriptors, but they are also bricks in a protective wall. It felt safer to hide behind a paragraph of text than it did to subject our family to a judge's scrutiny.

"Best interests of the child" is a legal test used to inform decisions about which caregiving and custody arrangements will best protect a child's safety, security, and well-being. Mothers were historically given preference over fathers in child custody disputes. With the emergence of no-fault divorce in the 1970s, "best interests of the child" became the standard instead of maternal preference.[47] This disadvantaged lesbian mothers exiting straight marriages, whose queerness marked them as unfit to parent.

What's in a child's (or children's) best interests is determined on a case-by-case basis, with courts often interpreting "best" against heteronormative and mononormative standards, with Black and Brown, disabled, trans, sex-working, and poor parents subject to even greater scrutiny. Historically, judges were often concerned with whether gay parents would raise gay kids.[48] Parents "who could, and were willing, to pass as straight were seen as acting in the best interests of their child[ren]," while those perceived as militantly queer were assumed to be harmful.[49]

When the American Psychological Association declassified homosexuality as a mental disorder in 1973, "courts no longer had a categorical basis for casting homosexual parents as inherently unfit."[50] Instead, judges required evidence of harm. Queer parents relied on expert witnesses to help prove their case, though they at first grappled with a lack of supporting evidence demonstrating their fitness to parent. This catalyzed the creation of a body of research intended to show that children raised by LGBTQ+ parents would suffer no ill effects.

"An academic consensus quickly developed that there was 'no difference' between children raised by queer parents and those raised by heterosexual parents," writes historian Erin Gallagher-Cohoon.[51] These studies emphasized that the children of LGBTQ+ parents were likely to grow up straight and gender normative, which was presented as a positive outcome. US marriage equality cases subsequently marshalled this evidence, submitting lists of approximately 150 studies showing that children of queer parents fared as well as those raised by straight people.[52] "Movement leaders also selected a disproportionate number of mothers and fathers to serve as plaintiffs in their cases," writes legal scholar Marie-Amélie George, explicitly excluding "less mainstream movement members, like flamboyant drag queens and sexual nonmonogamists, who drew attention to the ways in which members of the LGBT community defied convention."[53]

Several months after my encounter at the police station with Turquoise Sweater, I dreamed we had a new neighbour. She was a friendly white woman in her sixties who made an effort to get to know us. She seemed warm, but I didn't trust her. My suspicions were confirmed when my dream self figured out that our new neighbour was planning to report us to child services for being queer and affirming our children's genders. Her kindness was a facade to get closer to us to gather evidence we were harming our kids. I showed our new neighbour my own smiling mask, not wanting to let on that I knew what she was up to. When the moment presented itself, I snuck off to warn my co-parents so we could protect ourselves from the coming attack.

I am vigilant to the possibility of someone threatening my family, even in my sleep.

I sometimes worry that our children will feel othered by our family's differences. Sasha rolls her eyes when we ask her if she knows what "queer" means. "Yes!" she says, exasperated. "You talk about it all the time!" We live openly as a four-parent family and have supportive relatives, friends, teachers, and child care providers. We are unfailingly kind, polite, and grateful to them—always grateful. It is genuine: We feel thankful when people are nice to us and don't treat us like freaks.

When Sasha first started kindergarten, I was anxious about her looking put together for school: a nice-enough outfit, no holes in her pants, hair tidy and under control. I thought it would prove to her teachers that we took good care of her. I thought it would help them to see her, and us, as worthy of their regard. My anxiety about Sasha's appearance became a minor source of friction between my co-parents and me. They tended to have a more relaxed attitude about how the kids looked, while I hid the ripped leggings in the back of the closet and bought colourful scrunchies in an effort to entice Sasha into ponytails.

I am the only person in our family who grew up poor and was raised by a single mother. Perhaps this is why I have a heightened awareness of other people's eyes on my family. Perhaps this is why something in me is driven to prove that we are good. I am afraid of what might happen if we show our secret selves to the wrong person: Turquoise Sweater. The nasty neighbour from my dream. The first grader who asked my daughter if she was friends with the devil after one of her visibly queer parents joined their class field trip.

I want my children to know the history of where they came from and what is at stake for our family, without carrying the weight of my nightmares for what could happen if we aren't careful enough. I want them to grow up proud of being loved by so many people, to trust that they will always be cradled by many hands.

The sun sets early this close to the new year, so it was already dark at 5:30 p.m. when we sat down to eat. We had received approval of our guardianship application by email that morning, but we waited until dinner to tell the kids. We wanted the whole family to be there when we shared the news.

"We're your parents now," Nic said, smiling at Sasha, Corin, and Alder from her place at the table.

"We've always been your parents," I interrupted.

"I was going to say that," Nic said, sighing at my impatience.

We fumbled through a toddler-friendly explanation of what exactly we were celebrating. How do you tell a child that nothing is different except hopefully they are a little safer than they were yesterday?

The kids bumped their pink-and-orange plastic cups against our water glasses as we toasted Nic's and my new status as their official guardians. It felt a little strange celebrating something so pragmatic, but it was a relief knowing we wouldn't have to go to court, and our children love the ritual of clinking glasses. To them, the pleasure is in the gesture.

Becoming a parent has been the greatest surprise, and the greatest joy, of my adult life. My relationship with my children and my role in their lives is a conscious daily choice. It is a practice of fierce devotion not rooted in blood or law. An injustice of childhood is that you don't get to choose your parents or caregivers. Only my children can judge if I have acted with their best interests in mind. My commitment is to be worthy of them.

Sworn or affirmed before me at [city]**, British Columbia, on** [date]**.**

DOLLY, DORALEE, MY MOTHER, AND ME

I slid two photographs into an envelope addressed to my mother. When she opened it, the first thing she saw would be a picture of a homemade chocolate cupcake decorated with blue icing, the words "fancy lady" piped on it in pink cursive.

Under the sugary concoction was a photo of me, her twenty-four-year-old daughter, wearing nothing above the waist but a strategically placed pair of black electrical tape *X*'s. I have matching *X*'s stencilled in blush below my cheekbones, my mouth a slash of scarlet. Hands on hips, my bare belly milk pale against black-velvet hot pants, I stand confident in the knee-high red-leather boots I bought with the prize money from an essay on mothers who murder their children. My eyes drill into the camera, daring you to look.

The photo was taken in the living room of a new friend, a drag queen who invited me to go-go dance for a queer punk band whose slogan was "We're queer and we're recruiting." My fellow dancers were punks and drag queens, sex workers and riot grrrls, poets and activists. Boldly queer and unashamedly sexy, they telegraphed an energy that was both *Fuck you!* and *I know you want to fuck me.* Their teased-out wigs, torn fishnet stockings, and platform stilettos were an education in femme aesthetics. I didn't know I could be queer until they gave me the language for who I was and the courage to say it out loud.

On the back of the cupcake picture, I wrote of wooing a girl I had a crush on with talk of feminism in the academy. The girl, Leila, would become my first queer love. In October 2003, when I sent my mother the photos, I felt both worldly and hopelessly brand new. I was grown up enough to have moved across the country for grad school, where I was almost finished a master's degree and just beginning to call myself "queer" and "femme."

My femmeness was obvious to me in retrospect. I had always loved dolls and evening gowns, and as a girl I'd once fired my mother for not being enough like Dolly Parton. I took comfort in the continuity, but it seemed to confuse my mother, who was my closest confidante and the first person I came out to. Our relationship had been strained in the months since I emailed her from a university computer lab, declaring my new-found sexuality.

Her reply to my coming-out email included the line "But you used to play with Barbies when you were little!" The iconic blond doll that I had coveted in childhood was a stand-in for all the ways I didn't conform to my mother's idea of what a lesbian looked like. Perhaps she would have been more receptive to my announcement had I been a tomboy. But I rejected the Tonka trucks and combat boots she gave me in favour of a doll-sized hot-pink convertible and a child-sized pair of black-velvet Mary Janes trimmed in silver thread. I may have dated boys in high school and university, but girlness was my most enduring love.

My mother's reaction to my coming out was a turning point in our relationship. I had never felt so rejected by her before. We fought for weeks, eventually making up by mail. She extended the first olive branch, a postcard with an illustration of a baby frog sitting on a big green frog's back and the message "Honest to God, you can tell me anything. I promise to be a better listener and to get more modern. Don't forget, a horse used to bring ice to my childhood home, and TV was barely invented. Love you madly, Mom."

The envelope with two photographs in it was my peace offering, and a test. We lived thousands of kilometres apart and only saw each other a few times a year. This glimpse into my new queer world would prove just how accepting she really was. My upbringing had been steeped in her feminist values, which I still held close. Could she see this version of me as evidence of who her mothering had enabled me to become? Was she capable of celebrating me coming into my power as a femme? I feared all she would see was a young woman duped by the patriarchy into taking her top off for an audience.

I ran my tongue along the flap, sealing the envelope, then dropped it in a mailbox before I could change my mind.

My mother's feminism was the water I swam in as a child, yet something in me was always reaching for more: a sunken treasure or a sparkle on the surface, almost within my grasp. I kept reaching until queer femmes showed me I was possible. My mother gave me my name, but it was femmes who mothered me into naming myself.

Before I had femmes, I had Dolly Parton, a divine figure second only to Barbie in a pantheon of blonds whose lesser gods included Smurfette and Dee Snider, the lead singer of Twisted Sister. Dolly was like a Barbie doll come to life, and somehow more. Barbie was smooth, plastic, and pliable, most certainly a good girl. Dolly was all curves and carnality. With her voice and talent, she could have chosen a more subdued aesthetic. Instead, she went big: big hair, big breasts, a big smile, and an endless wardrobe of tight, bright, bedazzled outfits.

Dolly seemed perpetually in command of her power, even when she was playing a secretary in *9 to 5*. As a celebrity, she embodied everything I aspired to—wealth, glamour, an endless supply of rhinestones—while conveying a folksy charm that made her seem more approachable than other stars. My own mother favoured a more utilitarian aesthetic. I wished for a mother like Parton who was fluent in beauty—not the prim and proper kind, but the kind that grabbed you by the throat with its confidence and sex appeal.

As a girl, my favourite dress-up clothes were the evening gowns my mother sometimes let me buy from the second-hand store. One was floor-length red satin with floral panels. I would put it on and twirl, the skirt belling out as I grew dizzy, the fabric whispering its secrets to me as I spun. Another, ivory satin with puffed sleeves and silver trim, I called my "Cinderella dress." I awoke one morning to find it hanging from my canopy bed as if cut from my dreams. My mother had sewn it for me while I slept. She indulged my penchant for femininity, to be sure, but she didn't share it. Perhaps she hoped it was only a phase.

My mother, who as a girl had coveted her younger brother's Lone Ranger mask and silver toy pistol, tried resisting my obsession with Barbie. I eventually wore her down.

"I want a Barbie birthday party," I told her.

"What's that?" she asked.

"It's a party where everyone who comes brings me a Barbie."

To counterbalance the dolls and dresses, she gave me *The Paper Bag Princess* and *Free to Be... You and Me*, whose heroines were eager to shed the trappings of girlhood. To them, even a burned paper bag was better than looking like a princess. In the feminist children's literature of the early 1980s, femininity was portrayed as a quality liable to make you selfish, soft, and easily cowed by men—or get you devoured by tigers.

When I was older, but not by much, my mother told me true stories about men who hurt girls and women. She was trying to prepare me for the future she assumed I would inherit as a heterosexual woman surviving in a man's world. She was intimately aware of its perils. My mother's feminism was that of a woman who had looked the monster in the eye and survived.

Mine was that of a queer girl who didn't yet have words for who she was.

It's December 1980. My mother, the single parent to an eighteen-month-old, is enjoying a rare night off at the movies. The theatre is packed with women and a scattering of men, who sink lower in their seats the more loudly their wives and girlfriends laugh as the women onscreen enact elaborate fantasies of killing their boss, or suspend him from his bedroom ceiling, where he dangles like an irate pinata. The men glance warily around the theatre, its atmosphere sizzling with pent-up rage. Have women always been this angry?

Released just before Christmas, *9 to 5* was the second-highest-grossing film of 1980, its $103 million in box office revenues outstripped only by *The Empire Strikes Back*.[1] In it, Parton plays Doralee Rhodes, secretary to a sleazy corporate vice-president named Franklin Hart Jr. (Dabney Coleman). Her hair is a perfect cloud of platinum curls, her nails inch-long pink acrylics, her outfits somehow modest while relentlessly drawing attention to her figure. People dismiss Doralee as a dumb blond, but underneath her Southern drawl and sweet disposition is a savvy working woman with a pistol in her purse.

Parton's co-stars are Lily Tomlin as Violet Newstead, a tough-talking, hyper-competent single mom sick of training the men who steal her promotions, and Jane Fonda as Judy Bernly, a prim divorcee new to the workforce after her husband left her for his secretary. Violet is always doffing her blazer for a loose, boxy silk jacket, while Judy has the aura of someone who feels naked without a girdle and pantyhose.

When we first meet Doralee, she is unflaggingly kind to her co-workers despite them ostracizing her because they think she's a slut. "Rumour has it she's banging the boss," Violet whispers conspiratorially on Judy's first day. Both women are quick to believe office gossip about Hart and Doralee's affair—a false rumour we later learn originates with Hart as cover for his sexual harassment. Still stung by her husband's infidelity, Judy icily rebuffs Doralee's invitation to lunch.

Later, in Hart's office, Violet, who has just learned she was passed over for a promotion, accuses Doralee of being his mistress. Stunned by the revelation, Doralee's shock quickly turns to anger. She corners Hart, threatening to shoot him in the crotch if he doesn't leave her alone. Soon after, Judy watches Hart unjustly fire a woman for disclosing her salary to a co-worker.

The trio converge at a local bar, where they compare notes on their awful boss, whom they agree is a "sexist, egotistical, lying, hypocritical bigot." The night ends with them smoking a joint from Violet's teenage son. High on Maui Wowie, the women raid Doralee's fridge, then sprawl around her living room fantasizing about revenge. Their fantasies include hunting, shooting, poisoning, catapulting, lassoing, and roasting Hart over an open fire.

Doralee, Judy, and Violet's bond is sealed the next morning when Violet accidentally spikes Hart's coffee with rat poison. He survives, accuses Violet of trying to kill him, and threatens to call the police. A widowed mother of four, Violet is afraid of what could happen to her children if she goes to prison. To protect her, the women hold Hart captive in his mansion for six weeks while gathering evidence that he's been stealing from the company. They take advantage of his absence to forge memos to equalize salaries, relax the office dress code, open a workplace daycare, and implement a flexible work program.

Throughout, Doralee keeps her cool when confronted with circumstances that send Violet and Judy into a panic. After Violet steals a dead body from the hospital in an attempt to cover up the poisoning, it's Doralee who returns it, calmly proclaiming, "It's been taken care of," as she squeezes into the front seat of Violet's powder-blue Buick Skylark.

When I watch this scene now, it makes me think of a tweet by writer SC Dillon: "A butch will help you move. A femme will help you move a body."[2] It's no wonder I see myself in Doralee, the film's most femme-coded character. Violet, a straight woman played by the only dyke in a starring role, reminds me of my mom.

My mother sat at the edge of my twin-sized four-poster bed, arranging the rainbow-striped blue comforter around me. Sleeping under a white ruffled canopy made me feel like a princess. The pale eyelet fabric gleamed in the street lights that shone through our apartment windows. My Barbies slept nearby in the painted plywood bookshelf I used as a makeshift Dreamhouse.

The lace-edged collar of my worn flannel nightie peeked out from under the blanket as I snuggled deeper into bed. My long, dark hair was loose, its waves freed of the neat braids or ribboned high ponytails that held it back all day. I loved the sensation of the brush against my scalp each morning as my mother helped me get ready for kindergarten. Her hair used to be the same length as mine, but it was short enough now to skim her earlobes. "That's not my mummy!" I'd shouted when she picked me up from school with her new haircut.

I propped myself up on my elbows so I could look my mother in the eye, inhaling like I was about to jump off the highest playground tower before opening my mouth to speak.

"I'm sorry, but I'm going to have to fire you," I announced.

"Oh," she said. "That's too bad. I've really enjoyed being your mother."

She paused to contemplate her less-than-stellar performance report. I could smell the familiar mix of patchouli, cigarette smoke, and coffee that clung to her thrifted plaid shirt. I had never seen my mother in a dress, except in old pictures. Her everyday uniform consisted of loose shirts, soft twill pants, and red wooden clogs.

"Can I ask why you have to fire me?" she said.

I hugged Buster, my floppy-eared stuffed dachshund, to my chest, his body pancake flat from years of cuddling. If you looked closely enough, you could spot the tiny, even stitches where my mother had repaired a hole under his right arm.

"You're just not the kind of mother I expected," I replied.

"What kind of mother did you expect?"

"Someone more like Dolly Parton."

"I see." She was composed as she took this in, though a smile hinted at the corners of her mouth. "Can we talk more about this in the morning?" I nodded. "Sweet dreams, Zenie," she said, hugging me goodnight. "I love you."

"I love you too, Mom."

She switched off the lamp, closing my bedroom door behind her.

I lay in bed, silvery light slanting through my windows like a spotlight as I pictured myself and Dolly in matching hot-pink sequin-and-rhinestone dresses. I fell asleep dreaming of us cradled in the palm of a limousine's soft leather seats.

---

9 to 5 was inspired by Fonda's friendship with labour organizer Karen Nussbaum, whom she knew through their involvement in anti–Vietnam War activism. Nussbaum co-founded 9to5, National Association of

Working Women in 1973. Their mission was to organize clerical workers to fight workplace inequities, harassment, and discrimination, part of a larger feminist labour movement focused on ameliorating conditions for women workers.[3]

Dubbed "Hanoi Jane" for her contentious 1972 trip to Northern Vietnam, Fonda was surveilled by the FBI and the CIA for her anti-war activism and support of the Black Panther Party. Undeterred, she used her production company, IPC Films, to make movies with political themes. Before *9 to 5*, she starred in and produced the Vietnam War drama *Coming Home* (1978) and *The China Syndrome* (1979), a thriller about a cover-up at a nuclear power plant.

During filming, Fonda played host to a 9to5 staffer named Janice who had temporarily relocated from Boston to Los Angeles.[4] Janice was on-set every day to ensure *9 to 5* accurately reflected their members' experiences—and their demands. Central among these was showing how clerical work could be made better and how bosses were responsible for women's poor labour conditions. Fonda held rallies for working women in cities across the US before and after *9 to 5*'s release, often wearing a pink T-shirt that read "Raises, not roses."[5]

At a meeting with forty clerical workers arranged by Nussbaum's organization while the film was in development, a member of *9 to 5*'s creative team asked the women, "Have you ever dreamed of getting even with your boss?" Nussbaum recalled in a 2019 interview. "And the place lit up."[6]

"Yes, I remember one woman said she imagined cutting up her boss and putting him into the coffee grinder. And then making drip coffee out of him," Fonda added. "Another fantasized about breaking his knees with a bat as he walked by. Some [of their] fantasies were so violent we couldn't possibly use them in the movie."[7]

A high school graduate who could type a hundred words a minute, my mother got her first secretarial job at eighteen and did clerical work on and off until her early thirties. In the mid-1960s, her supervisor at her first job—an older woman I picture as Roz, Hart's uptight administrative assistant and self-appointed office snitch—would line up her subordinates for inspection, pinching their bottoms to ensure they were wearing their mandatory girdles.

In the late 1970s, my mother was hired as a secretary at the Canadian Broadcasting Corporation (CBC) in Halifax, Nova Scotia. Her boss was sexually harassing her, she told me, and she wanted him to stop.

"So I went to the army surplus store and bought a dead grenade," my mother said. "Then I took it to work and rolled it through his open office door."

It was the last time my mother ever worked as a secretary. That she wasn't arrested for this stunt says something about the era and the protective power of white womanhood. When I think about this story now, I wonder if, when watching *9 to 5* several years later, she was remembering the sensation of a grenade in her hand.

I was eight when she learned that Sheila Jones, a woman she had worked with in Halifax at the CBC, was stabbed and bludgeoned to death by her husband on their wedding anniversary. After killing his wife, the man died by suicide, leaving their two-and-a-half-year-old son alone with his parents' bodies for several days.

We lived in Ontario by then, so my mother channelled her grief for Sheila into a piece of memorial art. Her handwritten script, a concisely brutal account of how Sheila died, was superimposed over a black-and-white portrait my mother had made of her in the 1970s. In the photograph, Sheila, with shoulder-length blond hair and glasses, sits in a chair looking directly at the camera, one leg crossed over her knee. I remember seeing it in an art gallery as a third grader and thinking she looked kind.

My mother didn't hide from me how Sheila died. The women of *9 to 5* may have fantasized about murdering their boss, but my mother had no illusions about what we were up against in real life. While I had *The Paper Bag Princess*, *Free to Be... You and Me*, and Barbara Cooney's 1982 paean to self-determined spinsterhood, *Miss Rumphius*, my mother collected books on rape, sexual abuse, and violence against women.

She knew the most dangerous predators weren't in movies or storybooks. They lived among us: husbands, fathers, neighbours, bosses. Becoming a heterosexual woman wasn't my destiny or a God-given duty. It was an inherited burden she would teach me to bear.

It was Fonda's idea to cast Parton in *9 to 5*. She heard her song "Two Doors Down" on the radio while driving and laughed as she pictured her typing with her long acrylic nails.[8] She reached out to Parton, who had been looking at film scripts, to offer her the part.

With her conservative country music fan base, Parton took a risk by working with Fonda. Yet she saw in *9 to 5* an opportunity to break into the mainstream. Parton had dreamt of fame since she was a girl growing up poor in Tennessee's Appalachian Mountains. By 1979, she was an acclaimed country singer-songwriter, television personality, and savvy businesswoman seeking to broaden her audience.

Parton took the role of Doralee on condition that she also write *9 to 5*'s theme song, composing the film's titular anthem on-set between scenes. She used her nails as an instrument, at times accompanied by hairstylists clacking their brushes to the rhythm. The song, which was her first to reach number one on both the Billboard Hot 100 and the Adult Contemporary charts, went on to win a Grammy and was nominated for an Oscar. The album credits for "9 to 5" include "Nails by Dolly."

Film critic Roger Ebert called Parton a "natural-born movie star" in his review of *9 to 5*, likening her to Marilyn Monroe.[9] The film propelled her into the cultural mainstream. After *9 to 5*, she starred in the 1982 musical comedy *The Best Little Whorehouse in Texas* and had another chart-topping hit with "Islands in the Stream," her 1983 duet with Kenny Rogers. By 1986, she had opened her own theme park, Dollywood, near her hometown in Tennessee.

In the epilogue to *9 to 5*, Doralee's happy ending is quitting her secretarial job to become a country singer. For Parton, already a country star, the film was a launching pad to even greater celebrity and business ventures that would make her a multi-millionaire.

Parton's ascent to mainstream stardom after *9 to 5* coincided with my early childhood. She was so culturally ubiquitous that I don't remember the first time I saw her onscreen. She became an avatar for my hopes and dreams. As Tressie McMillan Cottom writes, Parton "made ambition about achievement, rather than inheritance."[10] Perhaps by having her as a mother I could become someone else.

My mother was a year younger than Parton, who was born in 1946. To me, they had little else in common, which was central to Dolly's allure. I was a child the first time I watched *9 to 5*, which, like *The Paper Bag Princess* and *Free to Be... You and Me*, would have fit within my mother's canon of acceptable feminist texts. Not every mother would allow her daughter to watch a PG-rated film about three women kidnapping and almost killing their boss. Mine's version of parental guidance was teaching me to survive in a society run by men like Hart.

She gave me a gendered and sexual education for the world she knew, one in which I must always be vigilant to the threat of male violence. Femininity was okay for toys or dress-up, but it could become a weakness or a distraction if I wasn't careful enough. When I look back on our relationship, I see my love of rhinestones, dresses, and dolls as my first act of gendered self-determination. Figures like Parton were a bridge to a future I didn't yet have language for, my affinity for Doralee an unspoken queer desire.

For all her feminism, my mother didn't teach me I could be a lesbian, and she certainly didn't teach me I could be a femme. Her generation was taught that girls should aspire to marriage and motherhood, and queer people could be arrested, fired, rejected by their families, and subjected to forced treatment meant to "cure" them of homosexuality. While my upbringing wasn't overtly homophobic, my mother wasn't equipped to raise me outside of the heteronormative paradigm that defined her world view.

We both assumed I would grow up straight. I had crushes on girls starting in elementary school, but I didn't consider my feelings for them romantic. Drawn to girls I thought were skinnier and prettier than me, I assumed the intensity of our friendships was powered by my desire to be like them, not my desire for them. I was a preteen before I knew that sex between women was possible, and I learned about it from fiction.

In grade 11, I met Peter, who became my first love. Both virgins, we decided to have sex after dating for several months. My mother, who didn't want us sneaking around, gave me permission to use my bedroom when I told her about our plans. Peter brought me a bouquet of red roses. I lit candles to set the mood, dressed in a lace slip. We were tender and a little fumbling with each other, full of wonder at what our bodies could do.

I was so focused on losing my virginity that I didn't think of my mother down the hall, poised to intervene if she heard me cry for help. I only felt lucky to have a mother I didn't need to lie to and the gift of a first time so different from the rape stories I had been raised with.

As a young person in the 1980s and 1990s, my gendered and sexual horizons were limited by what I saw around me at home, at school, and in popular culture. What I saw was predominantly straight. The only queer people I knew as a teenager were my friend's older brother and a local gay activist. By university, my circle of acquaintances had expanded to include a bisexual raver girl with spiky hair and facial piercings and two middle-aged lesbian professors from different departments whose androgynous wardrobes mystified me with their sameness. The only femme I had ever seen was in a documentary about lesbian history.

I had never met a queer person who resembled me. I understood my sexuality in the simplest of terms: I looked like a girl, so I must be straight. It was only by moving to Vancouver, where I met a community of femmes, that I became capable of seeing who I was.

Parton was nine when she met her best friend, Judy Ogle. "I'm sure many a maid in many a hotel has wondered why Judy and I will leave a double room with only one bed slept in," she wrote in her autobiography, *Dolly: My Life and Other Unfinished Business*. "We have always slept together since we were kids ... I don't like to sleep alone, never did." Their sleeping arrangements stoked rumours of a lesbian love affair, but "we've never been lovers," Parton said, "just good old pure, sweet, fun-loving friends."[11]

The friends enjoyed all kinds of fun over the years. The scene of Doralee threatening Hart with a pistol in *9 to 5* was inspired by a trip they took to New York in the late 1960s. Both women, then in their twenties, carried .38-calibre handguns for protection. When they got to the city, they teased their hair, put on tight skirts and makeup, and made their way to one of the city's porn theatres.

After exiting the theatre, a man aggressively propositioned Parton, assuming she was a sex worker. When he grabbed her "in places I reserve for grabbers of my own choosing," she pulled out her gun, shouting, "You touch me one more time, you son of a bitch, and I'm going to blow your nuts off!"[12] Ogle, who had recently been discharged from the Air Force, stood by laughing and smoking as Parton scared off the drunken man.

When they got back to their hotel, the women found their luggage in the hallway. Although Parton was a recording artist who had already begun appearing on *The Porter Wagoner Show*, hotel management didn't recognize the country star. They mistook her and Ogle for sex workers, evicting them from their room. The women flew home to Nashville that night, vowing never to return to New York.

Though absent from *9 to 5*'s narrow view of gendered and sexual labour, sex workers are recurring figures in Parton's self-mythology. As a child, she says, she aspired to be like a woman from her hometown with "yellow hair piled on top of her head, red lipstick, her eyes all painted up, and her clothes all tight and flashy."[13] Townspeople called the woman, who was rumoured to be a sex worker, "trash." To Parton, a girl accustomed to the deprivations of rural poverty, she was "the prettiest thing I'd ever seen."[14]

Parton, whose net worth is now valued at $650 million, is strategic about the image she presents. Steacy Easton characterizes her performance of sex work as an "aesthetic abstraction solidified with money," one that ultimately separates her from her working-class kin.[15] Parton calls herself a "trash queen," yet her "performance of blondness is a very particular thread of race and gender and class," writes Tressie McMillan Cottom. Here, "blond is code for white. That code channels oppression and desire, beckoning only to exclude most of us."[16]

As a dark-haired white girl growing up on welfare, my childhood infatuation with Parton was one of sameness and difference. I could see just enough of myself in Dolly to dream that I might someday become like her. She was a means of breaking with my mother, who had failed to meet my expectations. I yearned for Parton's opulence and affluence and admired how she seemingly did it all without a man at her side, her husband, Carl, notoriously confined to the shadows.

Coming out as a queer femme gave my girlhood desires a more enduring home. It also catalyzed a process of politicization that separated me from my mother as I found community among radical queers, cultural workers, Leatherdykes, and sex worker activists who taught me to view sexuality as political in ways she couldn't. My mother gave me *The Paper Bag Princess* and *Free to Be... You and Me*. They gave me *S/He*, *Skin*, and *My Dangerous Desires*.

One of the last conversations about politics I remember having with my mother before she died took place in December 2013. The Supreme Court had just deemed some of Canada's laws against sex work unconstitutional, marking a victory for sex workers' rights.

"Basically, my friends are happy with the decision, and your friends are sad," I told her, summing up the case. "My friends are right, though."

"No, my friends are right," she replied.

Our conversation stopped there.

My mother and I had mended our relationship in 2003 after I came out to her, but it also marked the point at which I learned there were things we couldn't talk about. For a mother and daughter as close as we had been throughout my childhood and adolescence, these silences were shocking at first. They eventually became a habit.

I didn't tell her about my forays into BDSM and non-monogamy, and we mostly avoided talking about where our feminisms diverged. It seemed like the easiest way to avoid a fight. Deep down, I was afraid she would think I had been corrupted by the culture of sexual violence that she had dedicated herself to protecting me from.

There were thirty-two years and at least two waves of feminism between my mother and me. Queer, kinky, polyamorous, I wanted sex that felt like freedom. My mother, who had long since given up on men, was celibate for most of my life. We both eschewed normative sexuality in our own ways, yet while she was alive, I could only ever see sex, like gender, as something with the power to divide us.

In our mini version of the sex wars, I saw myself as the younger, more liberated daughter, able to embrace femininity and sex positivity, unburdened by her mother's traumas. I cast my mother as a warrior against sexual violence so singularly focused on protecting me that she lost sight of pleasure and the possibility I could be anything other than straight.

I became so convinced my mother couldn't see all of me that I forgot to see her as more than a fixed stereotype. While my ultimate goal was preserving our relationship—the opposite of firing her for my fantasy of an ideal mother—my silence robbed us of the potential to change our minds.

When my mother died, I was thirty-four and had been out to her for more than a decade. Everything she owned became mine. Death brings with it strange intimacies and unexpected revelations. As I was packing up her things, I found the topless photo of me in a box, folded inside a purple cardboard sleeve with "October 2003" written on it in black pen. It wasn't me who made the sleeve or wrote the date on the front. I recognized my mother's handwriting and her compulsion to preserve the ephemera of our relationship.

She had photos of me in almost every room of her apartment, even the bathroom, which I found simultaneously endearing and embarrassing. Unlike the other pictures that I sent her, or the snapshots she took on disposable cameras, I never saw the topless photo of me on display in her home. It wasn't stuck to her refrigerator in a magnetic plastic frame from the dollar store or pinned to the wall beside her computer. I didn't see it on the wooden shelf in her bedroom or hanging in view of the toilet. Instead, I found it in a box, hidden away like evidence I had done something wrong.

Yet this wasn't the only naked photo I found while packing up my mother's things. In another box, I was shocked to find an envelope labelled "Pregnant Photos" with three nude self-portraits of my mother inside. In the one that most resembles the topless photo of me, she stands naked, hands on hips, her bare breasts small and high like mine. Not visibly pregnant, a bushy thatch of pubic hair juts out below her belly. She wears her long brown hair in two high ponytails like a cheerleader's, her lips in a sexy pout.

Who was this version of my mother? I wondered when I saw it. *Who did she take this picture for?* I had never thought of my mother as sexy, and certainly not as someone who would have taken naked pictures. Later, when going through her papers, I found a piece of writing in which my mother pined for a man with whom "lovemaking was unreal." She wrote of waking with his feet in her hands, thinking they were his head and shoulders, their sex so deliriously pleasurable it turned her upside down.

Perhaps paradoxically, uncovering these revealing traces of my mother's sexual life surprised me with their opacity by showing me a version of her I had never thought to look for. Today, when I place the photos of us side by side, I see two women intent on documenting something important about who they are as gendered and sexual beings. I wish I knew more about what my mother, a talented photographer, was thinking when she captured this self-portrait. It can't have been that long after she quit her job with a grenade.

I am still learning new things about my mother a decade after her death. I only wish I had been brave enough to show her more of whom she enabled me to become while she was alive.

(M)OTHER

My mother lies in the bathtub, a wet face cloth folded over her eyes like a compress, long dark hair ribboning out around her head. She holds her breath and sinks under the surface, hearing nothing but the muffled sounds of water in her ears. Part of her is always alert to her daughter's cry. The apartment is quiet for now. With some children, a too-quiet house might be cause for alarm, but her daughter isn't the type to get into trouble when left unsupervised.

Her daughter's preschool teacher praises her industriousness and self-discipline. *Has having only one parent forced her to grow up too quickly?* my mother wonders. She lets the thought dissolve like Epsom salts in warm water. There will be time to worry about her failings as a parent later, after she has put her daughter to bed, washed the dishes, and packed tomorrow's lunch.

She swishes her arms around in the tub, relaxing her limbs. Her fingers uncurl from the grip she has been unconsciously holding. She is always holding something: dirty laundry, a grocery list, a discarded toy, an empty wallet, a crying child. She lets the water engulf her. For a moment, she feels weightless, untethered by need.

She feels the first can hit before she sees it: A round, heavy shape lands beside her in the water with a thunk, just missing her body. A flash of red near her hip, not blood but tinned spaghetti. She surges out of the water, damp face cloth falling from her eyes. Blinking, she sees her daughter silhouetted in the doorway, steamy air escaping around her. The girl's cheeks are flushed. Her brown curls, the same shade as her mother's, have broken free of their red-plastic barrettes. She wears a ferocious expression as she winds up for another throw.

"Get out and make my dinner!" yells the girl as she launches a second can into the tub.

My mother flinches as a can of peas skims her shin. A balanced meal, she notes with a flash of pride. Her nakedness doesn't feel like freedom anymore. It feels like vulnerability. There is nothing between her and this onslaught of need.

"Okay," my mother says, in the same voice she would use to calm a frightened animal. "Okay," she repeats. "I'm getting out."

She reaches for the worn blue towel hanging by the tub, wraps it around herself, then pulls the plug. Water swirls down the drain, leaving two damp cans in its wake. She picks up the cans, awkwardly cradling them with her left palm as she takes her daughter's small dry hand in her right one. Her fingers are a little pruney from being underwater for so long.

They walk together to the kitchen: mother, daughter, dinner. For the first few steps, my mother lets herself long for the sanctuary of the tub, swallowing back a wave of resentment that rises as she recalls her abrupt ejection. She shakes it off, turning her eyes toward the room where she will cook tonight's dinner wearing a towel.

She grasps her daughter's hand a little tighter, using her grip to telegraph the sureness of her presence: *I am your mother, I am here, and I will take care of you.*

She has to. There is no one else.

My children, who call me ZeeZee, have four parents but no mothers. Each adult in our family has their own reasons for opting out of motherhood, though we all do care work that could be called mothering. I am the only cisgender queer femme among us. Some might see my femininity and assume "mother" would slide onto me like a second skin, but the notion chafes at my most sensitive places.

I sometimes say I feel more like a dad, and not just because I wielded the syringe of donor sperm that helped conceive our daughter. My role as a parent affords me a kind of freedom I associate with fatherhood. To be a mother asks for more endurance, more bodily sacrifice, more selflessness than I am able to give. I wear my dadness like a windbreaker—an easier garment to put on or take off than the heavy cloak of maternality. If I were a dad, I'd be a cool dad, a fun dad, the modern, sensitive kind who is more involved in his children's lives than his own father yet still gets away with a less-than-equitable share of the parenting.

But I'm not a dad. As a woman with children I feel compelled to explain why I'm not a mother either, though I sometimes pretend to be. I don't want to admit that I am too selfish to be my children's mother, but it's probably true. I hold "mother" at a distance because I am afraid of being needed too much.

When I picture myself wearing the cloak of motherhood, I am flailing in an ocean, sodden garments dragging me down under churning waves.

I fear that if I say yes to "mother," it will subsume me.

I didn't dream of becoming a mother when I was a girl. I wanted to be a glamorous and successful career woman like Day-to-Night Barbie. 1985's original girlboss arrived in a box emblazoned with the slogan, "Beautiful suit becomes glamorous gown. Lookin' great at the office or on the town!"

Day-to-Night Barbie spent her days clad in a pink-velvet blazer and reversible pencil skirt, a sparkly pink bodysuit peeking out from under her jacket. I admired her can-do attitude and ability to pull off metallic-pink fuchsia as daywear. "We love working from nine to five," went the jingle, "but when the day is done, we girls deserve some fun!" At 5:01, she doffed her blazer, revealing the full chiffon skirt she'd kept hidden during business hours. After swapping her spectator pumps for a pair of stiletto mules, she was off to the club with Ken on her arm.

Unlike Barbie, who was designed to never get married or have children, I assumed I would eventually become a wife and mother. I yearned for the stability of a solidly middle-class life. Motherhood seemed an inevitable part of the package, as did a husband, but my primary motivation was escaping the poverty that trapped my mother and me.

In grade 3, my English teacher had our class fill out a thirty-one-question exercise in heteronormative prognostication titled, "What Will You Be Like?" My mother saved my completed questionnaire in a slim white binder with my elementary school report cards and copies of her carefully worded letters to my principals and teachers critiquing their educational policies and staffing decisions.

My answers to the questions about children, marriage, and work are a microcosm of my childhood aspirations:

1. Will you have six children or more? NO.

8. Will you graduate from college? YES.
9. Will you earn a lot of money? YES.
10. Will you be boss in your family? MABEY.

16. Will you have a big wedding? YES.

21. Will you marry more than once? NO/YES.

26. Will you be a good father or mother? YES.

28. Will you get very angry with your husband or wife? NO.

30. Will you stay at home every evening? NO.
31. Will you work after marriage? YES.

I had my eye on the prize: When I was six, I told my mother I was going to marry a lawyer. "I hope they let me live in the shingled shed in the back of their mansion," she quipped in a poem about my marital goals.

I wanted a husband who would bring home the bacon, but he would need to cook it too, because I wasn't going to be anyone's housewife. Having been raised on children's songs like "Parents Are People," *Free to Be ... You and Me*'s homage to egalitarian parenting, I was determined that my marriage would be a feminist union. My husband and I would have successful careers and a manageable number of children (definitely fewer than six). We would take turns being the boss. I would earn a lot of money, and I wouldn't be stuck at home with the kids every night.

I would have it all.

"Having it all" was a predominant cultural expectation of white women during my childhood in the 1980s, reinforcing the idea that white working women's identities would not be complete without motherhood, while Black mothers were demonized through racist stereotypes like the "welfare queen" and expected to labour inside white women's homes. As Amanda Brennan writes, "'Having it all' began with racism and the eugenic imperative for white women to continue having children."[1]

The phrase gained cultural momentum with Joyce Gabriel and Bettye Baldwin's 1980 book, *Having It All: A Practical Guide to Managing a Home and a Career*, which advised working mothers to save time by doing two things at once.[2] It was followed in 1982 by *Cosmopolitan* editor Helen Gurley Brown's *Having It All: Love, Success, Sex, Money, Even If You're Starting with Nothing*. I didn't read either book as a girl or young woman, but their influence permeated how I learned to define successful womanhood, even if I had never seen a woman "have it all" in real life.

Gurley Brown wasn't a parent, and she didn't give children much attention in her book. Under the heading, "Children—Part of Having It All," she writes, "Now it's time to mention *children*—which a lot of people feel are a serious part of having it all (I don't agree and never wanted any but you have your own ideas about *that*)."[3] Though her use of italics drips with disdain for children *and* people's opinions about her not wanting any, Gurley Brown nonetheless assures readers they can successfully raise kids and have a big job, as long as they have an incredible amount of energy and paid help at home.

She takes for granted that women striving to have it all will have the means and the willingness to offload some of their mothering labour to paid care workers. Here, Gurley Brown pulls back the curtain to reveal a vision of having it all that is contingent on other workers—often racialized women and migrants—taking up the care work that white women won't, or can't, do on their own.

As a young girl, I relied on my single mother to meet all of my needs. She relied on welfare to meet ours. Our version of having it all was not having to put back any of the food in our grocery cart because we couldn't afford it. I didn't know what I wanted to be when I grew up, only that I wanted my life to be easier than my mother's.

I pulled the bathroom door shut behind me, checking to make sure it was locked. Our apartment had two bathrooms, but my spouse and I mostly used the one attached to our bedroom. We moved in together two years ago when we got married and weren't in the habit of barging in on each other in the bathroom. I locked the door anyway.

I had used the toilet in the middle of the night often enough that I knew how to make my way around the small rectangular space without illumination. That day, I kept the lights off not as a challenge to my senses, but because I didn't want to see myself reflected in the large rectangular mirror above the vanity.

I could only execute my ritual in the dark, unwitnessed by even my own image.

I reached for the thick sage-green bath towel hanging from a silver rack mounted on the wall, folded it over twice, and pressed it to my lips. I let out a scream, tasting terry cloth as the fabric muffled my cries. I poured my rage and frustration into the towel: "*You want too much You need too much You're suffocating me It's not my job to take care of you Why won't you listen to me Why can't you see me Why can't you take care of yourself I'm so angry with you Why won't you leave me alone!*"

By the time I finished screaming, I was red faced and panting from the exertion of letting out everything I had been holding inside, all the words I felt unable to say to my mother and my spouse. The intimacies between us rendered me silent. I only knew how to be "wife" and "daughter" by boxing away the parts of me that wanted to be nurtured or felt capable of saying no. I only knew how to be "wife" and "daughter" by silencing the parts shouting to be heard.

I should have been satisfied: I had a happy enough marriage, a successful career, a beautiful home, and a wardrobe worthy of Day-to-Night Barbie. Sure, my mother was constantly careening between health crises and my marriage was built on a foundation of codependence, but I had it all, didn't I? Everything but children, that was, because the idea of parenting actual children was laughable on top of how responsible I already felt for my mother's and my spouse's well-being.

I used to be a girl who would burst into a bathroom, shouting her needs loudly enough for everyone to hear. How had I become a woman hiding alone in a dark room, muzzling her screams?

It was the only way I knew how to keep giving what was being asked of me.

I don't remember the first time I heard my mother tell the story of me throwing cans at her in the tub. The telling I recall most vividly happened when I was in my early thirties, around the same age my mother was when she had me. I was a career woman with no intention of having children, so it was easier to put myself in my mother's shoes than to empathize with my younger self.

As I listened to my mother, I pictured her trying to snatch a moment's relaxation in the tub. My child self's audacity shocked me. I heard a story of a mother capitulating to the needs of a spoiled, selfish child rudely demanding her attention. I couldn't see the child's hunger, or her hands too young to use a can opener or operate a stove. I couldn't picture myself as a little girl, playing alone in the dark as dusk fell, stomach rumbling so loudly she couldn't ignore it anymore.

"What did you do?" I asked my mother when she got to the part of the story where I shouted and tossed tins of food.

"I got out and made you dinner," she said. "I shouldn't have been in the bathtub at suppertime."

Her matter-of-factness surprised me. Wasn't she angry? Didn't I deserve some kind of punishment? I heard the story as one in which a child—me—made unfair demands of her mother and was rewarded with compliance. Her willingness to give me what I wanted seemed symbolic of something troubling about the dynamics between us. Hadn't she always been a little too easy on me?

I understand this story differently now that I have young children of my own. When they are hungry, my children cry out to be fed. Sometimes, there are tears or yelling, or they refuse the food I offer them. Sometimes, they throw it on the floor. Sometimes, they tell me they are not hungry because they want to keep playing, then I watch them unravel as their body's need for fuel overtakes them.

I often want to be doing something other than feeding my children or cleaning up after them or wiping their poopy butts. I let their needs eclipse mine, because I love them and it is my responsibility to care for them. Case in point: I stopped partway through writing this paragraph to help one of my kids look for a missing blue-plastic toy slug. Do I care more about a toy slug than my book? No, but it matters very much to me that my children learn to trust that I will respond to their cries for help.

Parenting demands watchful attunement to our children's needs. In my four-parent family, this vigilance is distributed and collectively held, as is the responsibility for meeting those needs. It is what makes it possible for me to parent without building up a murky sediment of resentment. I read other women's accounts of mom rage as barometers of unmet need. If I were a mother, I would be seething. The fact that I associate motherhood with an accumulation of unmet need says as much about me as it does about motherhood, but for me they are inextricable.

As a girl, I used to climb into my mother's bed when she was trying to nap. Instead of letting her rest, I would lift her eyelids with my tiny fingers. "Wake up, Mom!" I would say, peering into her half-shut eyes, my face pressed in close, my breath hot on her cheeks. Her tiredness didn't matter. My mother never seemed to resent that I depended on her for every aspect of my survival: food, clothing, shelter, safety, love, nurturance, comfort. Her letters and diaries chronicle the pleasure she took in mothering.

The fact that I expected her to respond positively when I demanded to be fed evidenced my trust in her, just as her need to escape into the bath signalled how much she was carrying alone. I wonder if single motherhood ever felt suffocating, or if she ever wished to break free of her responsibilities.

She never said so, though she grappled with trauma in ways that led to more temporary disappearances. The light of her attunement blinked on and off, yet I grew up certain I was the centre of her world. As I got older and became more aware of the violence she had lived through, I felt the weight of knowing my mother had kept herself alive for me.

We needed each other, sometimes too much.

A vendor at the farmers' market tells my six-year-old daughter, "Ask your mom if it's okay to take a sample." I glance from side to side, wondering where the mother is. My daughter looks up at me inquiringly. *Oh right, I'm the mom, sort of.* I don't owe this friendly stranger, who is just trying to sell us a bottle of blueberry-lemon shrub, an explanation—only my kindness.

"Of course," I say, smiling and nodding as my daughter steps forward to receive a tiny waxed paper cup of fruit-flavoured seltzer.

For a moment, we both pretend that I am her mother.

"Remember to say thank you," I remind her as she gulps down her drink. If someone is going to assume I'm a mother, I want them to think I'm a good one.

I feel like a fake when strangers mistake me for a mother, but I rarely correct them. My silence is sometimes a matter of safety and often a matter of ease. I hide behind the protection afforded by my white femininity. My presumed motherhood acts like a social lubricant, soft and slick enough to smooth the edges of my queerness.

At six, my daughter understands that it is sometimes easier to pretend than to explain who we are to each other. That she already knows this fills me with both sadness and relief.

The instinct to blend in can be a protective reflex, one that reverberates with my childhood memories of how my family—my crazy mom, my deadbeat dad, our poverty—made me feel like an outsider. I sometimes play at being a mother to shield my children from our queer family's difference being weaponized against them.

I sometimes do it because I'm afraid I'll wound them if I don't.

I tug at the hem of my damp blue-cotton T-shirt, trying to generate a breeze. My armpits are clammy from sitting for so long in our bathroom's muggy air.

The twins laugh as they slap their hands on the water's surface, shrieking with glee whenever someone gets splashed in the face.

"Keep the water in the tub, okay?" I say, ducking to avoid errant spray.

At two and a half, Corin and Alder are big enough to have almost outgrown shared baths. They compete for the tub's prime real estate: the spot closest to the white-mesh basket of bath toys or where they can stretch out on their tummy and pretend to swim. There is only room enough for one swimmer, which is fine until they both want to use the tub as a swimming pool.

"'Pace! I need 'pace!" they shout while jockeying for position. I referee from my spot on the bath mat. The twins are still learning where they end and the other begins, and how to navigate conflicting desires. We are teaching them to ask for space.

Their squabble ends as abruptly as it began. Corin swims happily while Alder sits in the coveted spot near the toy basket, squeezing water out of a hole in a green-plastic turtle. Their fine red hair wisps into curls at the nape of their neck.

"I'm Baby Sam," Alder says, pausing their game with the turtle to pretend to be our friend's five-month-old baby. "Are you my mama Nicole?"

Is it my imagination, or do I suddenly feel sweatier?

I hesitate for a beat, dabbing at my brow with a pale-pink hooded bath towel embroidered to look like a kitten, then say, "Yes, I'm your mama Nicole." Inside, I am a heart-shaped box of Mother's Day chocolates left too long in the sun, sentimentality and sharp-edged guilt swirling into a sticky mix of melted chocolate studded with nuts.

I'm not a mama, but it feels cruel to say no. Having four parents in our family isn't enough to completely assuage the fear that I am harming my children by refusing them a mother. Maybe a moment of pretending is insurance against denying them a lifetime of something more essential.

Alder holds my gaze with their big brown eyes, rewarding my answer with a tiny satisfied smile. I rest my chin on the edge of the tub. We lean toward each other, giggling as our foreheads touch. A toddler playing at being a baby with their parent who is playing at being a mother.

The word hung silently in the air between my lover and me. *Mommy.* I kept my expression neutral, aware that a subtle gesture—my eyes narrowing, the curl of my lip—might telegraph the disgust I wished I didn't feel. I tried pushing it away, but the thing inside was stronger than me. I was grateful for the shadows this dimly lit bedroom cast over my face.

I stiffened as my lover nuzzled their face toward my nipple, a question mark in their eyes. They seemed younger than they were five minutes ago. A wave of weariness washed thickly over me. I hadn't even turned thirty yet. Why did I suddenly feel so old? My nipples were one of the most sensitive places on my body, rosy pink conduits with a direct line to my clit. I almost always wanted my lovers' mouths on my breasts, but not that night.

I inhaled the scents of our bodies, trying to reignite my desire: the faint musk of mingled pheromones and sweat, a hint of the drug store deodorant all of the butches and mascs I was hot for seemed to wear, the familiar smell of my cunt, fresh and a little spicy.

I searched inside for a tender bud that might bloom in the face of my lover's desires. I found only a clenched fist.

I could say yes to a lot, but not to this.

I knew enough to know that I was being offered something precious, but not enough to know how to refuse without shattering it. I wriggled away, shifting positions so we were face to face, my chest pressing into theirs. Was using their body to shield me from their desire a betrayal? I tried to make my escape seem sexy, but we both knew what was happening, even if neither of us would say it out loud.

I hoped it didn't kill the mood.

Closing my eyes, I took my lover's mouth in mine and willed the energy between us to shift. I couldn't bear to look at the need in them. It felt so deep and vast I feared it might subsume me.

"I don't do mom stuff," I told another femme at the kink conference. "It's totally off limits." I was in my early thirties and immersed in the queer Leather and BDSM communities, where I had explored many facets of my desires.

Our conversation revolved around the parameters of our play with erotic archetypes: experience had shown I could be a Daddy or a girl, but never a Mommy. Being a Daddy felt natural—my father's absence had left me an emptier canvas on which to compose an erotic identity.

I couldn't even begin to sketch what Mommy could look like. If I had them, those desires were blocked off by a thick stone wall. The stones had names: My mother. My marriage. My mother. My marriage. My mother my mother my mother my mother. I was mothering my own mother, who was dying. I was mothering my spouse because it was the only way I knew how to be loved.

I had no more mothering left to give.

Being a Daddy felt freeing. As a femme, it was a pleasurable kind of gender fuck that gave me access to a swaggering, lustful, possessive power I didn't feel in my everyday life. As a Daddy, I took what I wanted. My hunger was welcome, encouraged. I never worried about being or needing too much. I let myself be bigger, shouldering through doorways, sitting with legs spread wide. My attention and the nurturance I offered alongside my ferocious desire were gifts I offered in reciprocity for the strength, vulnerability, and unbridled wanting my lovers showed me in return.

I wanted sex to feel like an escape, not a trap. When I tried to imagine myself as a Mommy, my boundaries became porous, care leaking uncontrollably out of every orifice. I built a wall to protect myself against a tidal wave of need.

—∞∞—

I have no siblings, so my mother was my only live-in playmate, but I set the rules. In a letter she wrote to a friend when I was six, she recounted how I became short-tempered and kicked her out of our game when she got Barbie's story wrong. I fantasized about having it all. My mother wanted to be taken care of.

The day I ejected her from playing dolls, I was acting the part of Day-to-Night Barbie, off to climb the corporate ladder in her pencil skirt and pink-and-white pumps. My mother was Ken. "While Barbie slammed desk drawers and rummaged through her briefcase," my mother wrote, "I had Ken lie down on the bed with his apron on." Later, Ken invited Crystal Barbie and Ken II over to drink wine and eat pizza. He rushed them out of Day-to-Night Barbie's apartment just before she was due back from work, hiding their dirty wineglasses beneath her unmade bed.

Barbie arrived home to find Ken wearing an apron but without dinner on the table. In my mother's version of the story, Barbie got mad at Ken for not saving her any pizza. She wanted dinner and dancing, not a helpless man and a messy house. Ken ruined Barbie's fantasy while I seethed at my mother for failing to go along with mine.

My mother had a different fantasy entirely: "I want Barbie to bring home the groceries and suggest places to go at night, then pay my way," she wrote. "I want to be 'Mom-med.' I haven't had a vacation in seven years." Was hers a queer desire—Day-to-Night Barbie as ideal provider and caregiver all wrapped in one—or was it that my mother couldn't imagine being nurtured by a man?

She knew a real mom doll, unlike Barbie, would never sell. "How boring to have real mom dolls," my mother wrote. "Their lips would move so they could complain about all the toys in every room of the apartment. They would cry and cover their heads with blankets when they ran out of money and the system turned against them."

In my mother's world, real mom dolls didn't have the energy to go out dancing after a long day at work. They were worn out by the labour of surviving. Real mom dolls didn't have it all; they had too much, and too little, forever seeking a balance that was just out of reach.

—∞∞∞—

While care and nurturance are a hallmark of my relationships with other queer femmes, no femme has ever expected me to mother them. I can't say the same about the masculine people in my life. This is indicative of gendered dynamics that extend beyond, yet are inextricably entangled with, the intimate and erotic.

A younger butch once wrote asking me to mediate a perceived conflict they and several of their peers had with a group of femmes over a song one femme had written called "Literally Anything Before Bros." The butch's message positioned me as the older, wiser, more reasonable femme—mommy being asked to referee a dispute among the children.

I declined.

I resented the assumption that I could be neutral in a debate over a femme's right to declare her allegiance to something (literally anything!) other than propping up masculine supremacy.

I also resented feeling like I was being asked to tidy up someone else's mess.

"I'm not your mom," I wanted to say. Instead, I wrote a reply graciously declining their invitation, probably starting with something like "Thank you for thinking of me." I did not, in fact, want them to think of me this way, but I also didn't want them to think I was a bitch (see also: mean mommy), so I held my tongue.

"People have both more entitled expectations of femmes' time and ears, and of femmes being perfect," writes Leah Lakshmi Piepzna-Samarasinha. "Expectations run high that you are either a magic mommy who fixes everything perfectly and infallibly and never says no, or you are a shit failure bitch who deserves every bit of rage thrown at you."[4]

No wonder so many femmes these days want to be Daddies.

I've been part of queer femme communities for more than twenty years and first started playing as a Femme Daddy in the early 2010s. Back then, the only Femme Daddy accessories I ever saw were sold by niche queer crafters at kink events. I remember coveting another femme's handmade rose fashioned from a hunter-green hanky. Today I can find an array of Femme Daddy–themed accessories for sale on Etsy, Amazon, and Instagram: Femme Daddy T-shirts, hats, tote bags, jewellery, mugs, key chains, and even throw rugs. There's "Hot Mom" and "Cool Mom" merch, but there is no similar array of readily available swag for the self-proclaimed Femme Mommies out there.

While there's a big difference between what femmes will announce with our accessories and what we might desire (and/or get paid) to do in the bedroom or dungeon, I'm curious what this cultural phenomenon signals about how queer femmes relate to Mommy and Daddy archetypes. Why *are* so many femmes keen to proclaim themselves Femme Daddies? Femmes are adept at purposefully reclaiming, remixing, and divesting from dominant notions of femininity, so my instinct is that there's more at work here than the ever-expanding universe of gendered and erotic identities femmes feel able to lay claim to.

Do Femme Daddies have more fun than Mommies? More power? Do they feel freer from non-consensual care work and emotional labour the same way real dads are? Does saying no feel easier as a Daddy than as a Mommy? It did for me.

In the essay "Mean Mommies: Care in Contemporary Queer Literature," author Jenny Fran Davis called Mommy "the patron saint of care and caretaking."[5] Mistress Danielle Blunt, a queer professional dominatrix whose specialties include Mommy play, moves between a range of caregiving archetypes in her personal and professional relationships. In a conversation about these archetypes, Blunt said, "Mommy wants to give you what you need and what you want. Daddy wants to take what's his."[6]

Blunt says she is drawn to Mommy play in part for the transformative possibilities it affords, yet emphasizes how its potential for healing attunement pivots upon consent. As a woman, care is expected of her; as a Mommy, Blunt is only going to "nurture and care for you in a consensual and negotiated way" within the bounds of scenes with a definite start and end point.[7] She is paid for her nurturance and care when she does so in the context of her professional role as a sex worker.

When I have been "Mommied" without my consent by lovers, partners, or acquaintances, whether erotically or relationally, it felt as if care were being extracted from me. The reservoirs of care I had access to in those interactions were always mediated by the care I was giving and receiving in different parts of my life. The prospect of embracing Mommy as an erotic identity felt as impossible to me as becoming an actual mother did in the era when I was in a locked bathroom screaming into a towel. I started identifying as a Daddy around this time because it made it easier and less complicated to ask for what I wanted and to set limits while playing with power and nurturance. This made it hotter.

I associated being a Mommy with feeling needed too much, so I reacted by shutting down those parts of me. I assumed I would feel this way forever.

I was wrong.

—∞∞—

My date and I had played together a few times. Whenever we met, I delighted in discovering something new about him: a tattoo on his thigh I hadn't noticed before, the way he shivered with pleasure when I ran my fingers along the sensitive flesh of his ribs, how when we kissed, the skin around his mouth smelled sweet and a little earthy.

The novelty of our intimacy wasn't just because we were in the early stages of getting to know each other. For months, the only naked body I had touched was my own. I had taken a break from sex and dating to grieve my mother and my marriage. Now summer had come, and my desires were waking up.

Late-evening sunlight slanted down on my date's face, his eyes half closed. I was lying in his bed on my side, using my right arm as a pillow. The skin around his lips was flushed from kissing, his chest red from when I had straddled him, smearing my wetness across his belly as I rained blows into the meat of his pecs. I reached out, stroking his cheekbone with my fingertips.

"Aren't you a beautiful boy," I said, cupping his chin.

I had never referred to him this way before. His small, pleased smile told me *boy* was a key that unlocked something in him.

I felt it too, a reciprocal opening. *Mommy* rose up in me, an energy so lush she was almost a third presence in the room. *I didn't know you were here*, I thought. *I've been here all along*, she told me. She filled every inch of my skin. I welcomed her in.

"Come here," I said, pulling my boy in close. "Come to Mommy."

I felt expansive, like there was room enough inside me for us both to rest for a while. Guiding him to my breast, I felt a wash of pleasure as he took me into his mouth.

I had to say no to Mommy before I could say yes.

That yes came only after death and divorce reshaped my life and whose care I felt responsible for. I became the primary locus of my care when I stopped dating or having sex for almost a year to grieve. During this time, I was held by a tight cluster of femmes and cared for by friends of all genders.

My status as a griever gave me the permission I needed to stop compulsively giving beyond my capacity. It eroded my resistance to being cared for. I still feared being needed too much, but grief, like BDSM, made me more adept at locating and naming my limits. I got better at asking for what I wanted, receiving help, and setting boundaries around what I would and wouldn't do for others. These skills translated into every facet of my life, including the relational and erotic.

Mommy emerged from this ground. Her sudden arrival surprised me—I didn't feel the stone wall inside me coming down, just who walked through the opening left behind when it fell. I took her presence as a measure of my healing. That I found a Mommy in me was a hard-earned and rare treasure.

The erotic was a container in which to experiment with being expansively nurturing without letting another's needs overwhelm me. Having clear boundaries helped: My lovers and I were consenting adults in pursuit of mutual pleasure inhabiting negotiated, time-bound roles. My erotic life offered me an escape from the everyday, but it was also a space for practising new ways of relating to my own and others' wants, needs, and care.

Refusing all forms of maternality was a strategy I used for years to protect myself against feeling flooded by others' needs. This changed when I became capable of embodying Mommy as an erotic archetype. It is why this essay can't simply be a repudiation of motherhood: I am never a mother, but I am sometimes a Mommy. As a queer person and a woman with young children, I am wary of juxtaposing my erotic identities with my role as a parent, particularly in the current socio-political climate. Fear kept telling me to write Mommy out of this essay, but I refused.

Queering our relationship to motherhood asks us to open up space around who a mother is and what mothering can be. It rejects the idea that the maternal must never live alongside the erotic. Instead of simply pushing motherhood away, like I did for so long, it is an invitation to become curious about what—and who—might live within us.

I ease my naked body under the water's surface, inhaling the faint scent of lavender bath salts as heat engulfs me. The water is hot enough that my pale skin flushes pink after several minutes of immersion. It is one of my nights off from cooking dinner or putting the kids to bed. As my co-parents run through our family's evening routines, I am blissfully alone with nothing to do but soak in the tub. I relish the pleasure of being unneeded.

Steam curls around the well-worn copy of Patrick Califia's 1988 book of queer BDSM erotica, *Macho Sluts*, that I hold in my left hand. I have read some of its stories so many times over the years that the paperback falls open to them like an index of my desires. *Macho Sluts* is out of print, old enough now that my copy feels like a precious remnant from a generation of queer elders and ancestors whose sexual lives laid a foundation for my own. I remind myself that some of them were parents too.

Reading it makes me nostalgic for an era of queer Leather culture I was too young to experience first-hand. Underneath is a longing for something deeper: I am nostalgic for the version of me whose life more closely resembled its stories. I spent nearly a decade jetting around to kink conferences before my first child was born. When I became a parent, my orbit grew smaller, my daily rhythms more oriented around the domestic. Even with multiple parents in our family, the demands of everyday life constrain my capacity for erotic exploration, as do the realities of navigating queer Leather spaces where I am at higher risk of bringing COVID home to my family.

While my desires remain those of a femme forged in queer Leather communities, I have barely played as a Mommy or a Daddy since becoming a parent. It wasn't a conscious decision so much as a shift in my ability to explore these facets of myself with other consenting adults. With so much of my daily life oriented around doing "mom stuff," I have less time and energy to devote to the erotic—particularly that which calls upon my reserves of attunement, deep presence, and care.

I put my book down with a sigh.

I love who I am now, but I miss who I used to be.

I dunk my head under the water, letting it hold me for a moment. Warm liquid envelops my face as I remember that nothing is static, including me. My longing for what once was lives beside curiosity for who I am still becoming. I trust that Mommy will come back when she is ready.

I wish I could listen to my mother tell the story again of when I threw cans of food at her in the bathtub. I would ask different questions than I did when I was younger, like: What did mothering mean to you? What did it teach you? What did you love about being my mother, and what felt hard? I would want her to know that I forgive her if she ever felt guilty for wanting to get away from me and her responsibilities, and that I'm sorry she had to hold so much alone.

I would tell her that I am no longer a woman who rejects all forms of maternality and who found her own path into mothering, if not motherhood. I would want her to know that my kids have dinner every night at 5:30 but it is not always my job to cook it. She would love to bear witness to the densely woven web of care that surrounds me. I wish I could weave her into it. Instead, I look for traces of her in her poems and letters, in my memories, and in how I mother myself now.

My mother's death was a rupture that created an opening; I passed through it and met the mother in me. I think of her when I sit down to write, or soak in the tub, or when I drop everything to find a lost toy. I think of her when I remember the girl I was who dreamed of having it all, and the woman I became, not mother but ZeeZee, sometimes Mommy, always seeking containers capacious enough to hold me and all of my care.

LOVE ME BACK TO LIFE

"You are entering the Love Party!" read the handmade neon-pink sign tied to the brown wooden fence. The wide double gate was propped open, giving guests a view of the bushy rhododendrons lining the northern perimeter of our yard. Only a few scraggly purple and fuchsia blooms were left this late in July, their waxy green leaves beckoning in the breeze.

To enter the backyard where the ritual and celebration would take place, everyone had to pass under a rounded brass arch. It was hung with fringed foil curtains from the dollar store, sunlight glinting off golden strands. A steady stream of soap bubbles effervesced from a borrowed bubble machine.

"It's like a portal!" someone said, and so it was. Kids and adults paraded through the arch, laughing and dancing as they crossed the threshold between everyday life and somewhere more magical.

Cognitive psychologist Endel Tulving used the term *mental time travel* to explain how memory allows us to mentally travel backward in time as well as into the future. "You can know a lot of things without mental time travel," said Tulving, "but you can't remember events from your past, or anticipate the future, without it."[1]

When I see her standing in my yard just after sunrise, we cry and hug for a long time. Her shape feels familiar but different. Before she died, her body was fragile, birdlike, all bone and sinew. This one feels sturdier, more vital. I can't remember the last time I saw her outdoors.

"I didn't know you were coming back," I say.

"I didn't either," my mother says. "You loved me back to life."

"Are you better?" I ask.

"It depends what you mean by better," she says. "I'm still me."

"Can you breathe?" I ask.

"Yes," she says, smiling. "I can breathe."

"How long can you stay?" I say.

"I don't know," she says.

We hold each other silently for a few moments, chests rising and falling together. I remember a time before memory, when the first sounds in my still-forming ears were her beating heart, the air in her lungs, the pulse of her blood in my umbilical cord.

A faded cotton bedsheet printed with apricot-coloured flowers was strung between two soaring fir trees. It declared, "QUEER LOVE IS SACRED AND INFINITE" in hand-painted block letters. The foot-high purple-and-pink glitter script glinted in the sun, announcing the intention at the heart of our ritual.

The ritual, a not-wedding we co-created with friends, would have many parts, each one amplifying the intention. We were gathered not to legally bind ourselves in marriage but in reverence for the love we felt for each other, our families, friends, and communities. Our party celebrated love in all forms. We wanted everyone to come away from it feeling cherished and more deeply woven into our relational web.

A few guests in bright summer clothes milled around a brown kraft paper chart taped to our house's weathered grey clapboard siding. They used different-coloured Sharpies to add themselves to the growing number of interconnected nodes mapping our connections. "Where did you first meet Riley and Zena?" read a hand-painted sign above the chart. Some of the nodes were "Queer!," "Femmes," "We're related," "Magic," "Sports," "Camp," "We lived together in a collective house," "We dated the same person," and "We're exes."

If they looked down, our guests would see the phrase *QUEER LOVE IS SACRED AND INFINITE* repeated behind them in purple paint on our concrete patio. It had seeped through the fabric the night before when Mars painted the banner, anchoring our intention into the ground beneath our feet.

Tulving coined the term *chronesthesia* to describe "a form of consciousness that allows individuals to think about the subjective time in which they live and that makes it possible for them to 'mentally travel' in such time."[2]

He recounts the case of a man he calls K.C., who developed amnesia after a traumatic brain injury. While K.C. was aware of present-day events, he lost his capacity for episodic memory—that is, he could no longer recall anything that had happened to him in the past. K.C. also lost his ability to imagine the future. For him, the past and future were both blank.

Episodic memory powers our chronesthetic capabilities. When we mentally time travel, we enter a state of consciousness similar to the one we were in when the memories were stored.[3] A familiar scent, like coffee, can transport us to a different time.

—∞∞—

Steam wafts from the pink-and-grey mug in my mother's hands. She lifts it to her lips, testing to make sure her drink isn't too hot before taking a sip. She closes her eyes, savouring the taste.

"Ahh," she says. "It's been so long since I had coffee. I miss it."

"They don't have coffee there ... uh, where you were?" asks Riley from their seat beside her at our long wooden patio table. "Sorry, I don't really know how all this works."

"That's okay," my mother says, chuckling. "How would you? You've never died before."

"Good point," Riley says.

"Things taste different when you have a body," my mother says, taking another sip.

Riley nods, drinking from their mug of Earl Grey tea. They pass my mother a plate of chocolate chip cookies. She takes two.

"I wanted to thank you," my mother says.

"For what?" Riley says.

"For taking such good care of Zena. I've been watching you the whole time."

Riley's eyes grow wide.

"Not like that," my mother says.

Riley exhales. They both laugh.

"I keep tabs on Zena," my mother says. "I like to know how my daughter is doing."

She pauses to eat a bite of cookie. "You love her how I always wanted her to be loved. I can tell she feels safe with you. She seems softer, more at home in herself."

My mother takes Riley's hand in hers.

"When she's with you," she says, "I see the amazing woman she's become, but I also see my little girl. Thank you for loving them both so well."

"Thank you for raising her," Riley says. "She talks about you all the time."

"I know," my mother says. "Do you have any cigarettes?"

"No," Riley says, "but I can pick some up for you. Menthols?"

My mother nods. "Might as well enjoy this body while I have it."

Sixty of us gathered in a circle under the shade of a huge canvas tent. Some people stood; others sat on the grass or on wooden folding chairs. Nic and Mars kept watch as the twins toddled around in hand-me-down tutus—Alder's flamingo pink, Corin's gold leopard print—and colourful floral T-shirts. Sasha sat cross-legged on the ground wearing butterfly wings, a flower crown, and a bright-blue dress made especially for her by Ollie, Riley's ex turned best friend.

There was no stage or altar. Riley and I held hands and stood alongside our friends and family. I wore a calf-length sundress with yellow, white, and pink flowers, sunflower-yellow heeled sandals, and a spray of fresh flowers in my hair. Riley wore a lightweight pink-and-blue paisley long-sleeved dress shirt and matching pink dress shorts.

Wherever I looked, I saw the faces of people I loved. Only my two oldest friends at the party had met my mother. To everyone else, she was a memory I had shared or a story they had heard me tell.

I felt her absence like an ache.

Our friend Lex, clad head to toe in neon-yellow linen and mesh, pulled several chunky balls of turquoise and fuchsia yarn from a cloth bag. Instead of an officiant, we had a rotating cast of queer witches, who each had a role in creating our do-it-yourself ritual.

"It's time to cast a circle," Lex said, "and I need your help. Can I get some volunteers?"

"Me! Me!" said the older kids, waving their hands. Lex passed balls of yarn to four girls in party dresses.

"Okay, magical helpers." The girls, ranging in age from four to nine, listened intently. "We're going to use this special yarn to knit all of us into a big web. We'll know the circle is open when everyone is touching at least one strand. Are you ready?"

The kids nodded enthusiastically, then fanned out under the tent with their yarn. I was surprised by how systematically they distributed it at first—when we planned the ritual, we had expected this moment to erupt immediately into joyful chaos.

"Toss it!" encouraged Lex. One of the girls threw her ball of yarn across the circle. Another followed suit. "Yeah," said Lex, a huge smile on their face. "Just like that!"

Soon we were all giggling and reaching for bright flashes of yarn as they streaked past, weaving an ever-denser network of connections to hold the magic of us.

"The ability to imagine our future, a new and unknown future that no longer includes our deceased loved one, seems to use a similar brain network as remembering our past," writes neuroscientist and psychologist Mary-Frances O'Connor in *The Grieving Brain*.[4]

We want to know where our loved ones are in space and time. Research has shown that we create mental maps to locate and keep track of them, encoding representations of our loved ones in our neurons. When we grieve, we are learning to live in the world without those whom we have lost, a process that literally rewires our brains.

My mother kneels on the grass, instinctively putting herself at child level. I recognize the thrifted navy-blue-and-green-plaid shirt she is wearing.

The kids are tentative at first, like they always are with unfamiliar adults. They peek out at her from behind Riley and Mars's legs, Alder clutching Nic's hand.

"This is your grandma Lynne," I say. "ZeeZee's mom. She came for a visit." Riley puts their arm around my shoulders, steadying me as I watch my mother meet her grandchildren.

"Hi," she says. "I'm your grandma Lynne. You can call me Lynne if that feels easier." She stays where she is, letting them know they can come to her when they are ready.

Her gaze roves from kid to kid, drinking in their faces, her eyes shining. I hold my breath, trying not to puncture the moment with a sob.

"You must be Sasha," my mother says, looking at my daughter. "I hear you're really good at building things."

Sasha beams. "I am," she says. "Want me to show you the camper van I made out of LEGO?"

"I would love that," my mother says. "And you must be Corin and Alder," she says to the twins, who have come out from behind their parents' legs and are moving closer to the grandmother they have met only in stories. "Did you know that we have the same birthday?" she asks.

"I'm sorry I haven't been able to come to your birthday parties. I live really far away. Should we have cake with dinner tonight and pretend it's our birthday?"

"Yeah!" says Corin.

"With candles?" says Alder.

"And ice cream?" says Sasha.

"And sparkles?" says Corin.

"They mean sprinkles," says Sasha.

"All of it," says my mother. "Let's have all of it."

The circle quieted to a hush as Lupin and Nour stepped into the centre. Lupin's short-sleeved blue-and-red-checked shirt and khaki shorts accentuated their long limbs, making them look extra tall beside Nour, who was three. Nour wore a navy-and-white-striped cotton dress with denim shorts underneath, her caramel-coloured skin burnished by the sun.

"Do you want me to pick you up?" Lupin asked in a quiet voice.

Nour nodded, suddenly shy at being the centre of attention.

Lupin scooped Nour into their arms, where she rested on their hip, holding a tiny brass bell in one hand.

"We are here and now together to celebrate the magic of queer love. We know that we're supported by those who came before us," invoked Lupin. "When Nour rings this bell, listen and feel the presence of your beloved ancestors—ancestors of blood, of love, of community. Feel them bless this commitment and celebration."

Nour rang the bell. Its clear tone called in those who had come before.

I pictured my mother stepping into the circle.

"And we are supported by our descendants," said Lupin, "all those who will come after us. When you hear the bell, listen into and feel the presence of our descendants of blood, love, and community. They are here too, blessing this commitment and celebration."

Nour rang the bell again. Our circle became infinite, past, present, and future resonating in the spaces between us.

When we grieve someone who has died, "the object of grief is not death *per se*, but *death as a loss of possibilities*," write philosophers Matthew Ratcliffe, Louise Richardson, and Becky Millar.[5]

If we understand grief as a process that unfolds temporally, it makes sense that "mental time travel allows us to juxtapose our past, present and future experiences and bring the loss of life possibilities to mind."[6] We experience emotions in the present when we recall the past or imagine a future without the person we lost.

Put simply, grief makes us into time travellers.

Sasha and I sit flanking my mother on our grey living room couch, looking at old photographs together.

"That's ZeeZee?" Sasha says, pointing at a picture of me grinning earnestly at the camera with long dark hair and a fruit-patterned dress, one hand raised in a wave.

"Yes, that's her," my mother says. "She would have been about a year older than you are now."

Sasha leans against my mother, glancing between me and the photograph as if trying to match the child's face to the adult beside her.

"I was in grade 2," I say. "And my teacher was so mean! I got in trouble for calling her a witch—that was before I knew witches were cool."

"Do you remember when you got sent to the principal's office for biting another kid?" my mom asks.

"Yeah," I say. "I bit him right on the butt!"

"On the butt?" Sasha says, erupting into giggles.

"On the butt!" I say. "I would do anything to protect my team's beanbags."

Still laughing, Sasha hops off the couch and says, "I'm going to go play *Minecraft* now."

She wanders downstairs to her video game while my mother and I stay on the couch flipping through photographs. I inch closer to feel her against me.

We find a black-and-white print of four-year-old me on my mother's lap, her arms wrapped around me, her lips pressing into my hair.

"I keep a copy of that one on my altar," I say. "Sometimes I talk to you. I wish you could talk back. There are so many things I want to ask, so many things I wasn't brave enough to say while you were alive."

"Why don't you tell me some of them?" she says.

"What if we run out of time?" A phantom clock ticks in my head, counting down to an unknown end point.

"We don't know how much time we have left," she says. "This is the time we have now. Let's make the most of it."

My mouth crowds with questions. What do you say to someone you've been grieving for a decade? What do you do with a second chance?

Riley and I stood face to face in the centre of the circle, preparing to read the love letters we had written for each other.

"Loving you is a delight," Riley said. "I love how enthusiastically you express your love for me by whisper-screaming because it would be rude to scream 'I LOVE YOU' right in my face."

We balled our fists and scrunched our faces in a spontaneous demonstration as we whisper-screamed "I LOVE YOU!"

"I love your dedication to community," Riley continued, taking my hand in theirs. "And I love the joy you take in children. I see how you carry your mom in your interactions with them."

Riley had never met my mother, but they could see how she lived on in me. In our first year of dating, they surprised me with a birthday scavenger hunt after I told them how my mother had started the tradition when I was a girl. Riley became a caretaker of my mother's memory. It was one of the things that made me fall in love with them.

I sniffled into a tissue, then took a deep breath to read my letter to Riley.

"I thought I knew how vast chosen family could be," I said, "then you came into my life and invited me into a whole new galaxy of possibilities.

"I tell people, get yourself a triple earth sign with a secure attachment style." Laughter rippled across the circle. Everything around us was alive. Birds sang in the distance; grasshoppers chirped; buzzing bees collected pollen from jars of homegrown dahlias, snapdragons, and gladioli. A chorus of beings called back to us, adding their voices to the love spell.

"You give me roots I didn't know I was capable of growing, and they're flourishing in the nourishment of your love and care," I said. "Many things have taught me to run, but you helped me learn how to stay."

Research shows that people living with complicated grief—clinically defined as a more intense and prolonged form of grieving—are more likely to "exhibit deficits in their ability to recall specific autobiographical memories" and less likely to imagine a future that does not include their lost loved one.[7]

Psychologists who study bereavement have catalogued reasons for remembering our dead. Among these are to maintain intimacy with them, to learn more about ourselves, and to connect with others and teach them about the past.[8] Remembering negative experiences with lost loved ones can be a means of processing and integrating those experiences into our self-view after the loss.

Remembering is a relationship.

Grieving rewrites the future.

I swallow, bracing myself for what I am about to say.

"I'm sorry," I tell her, "for destroying your archive."

My mother flinches. The air between us shifts as she pulls slightly away.

"It was my legacy," she says, studying her hands. "My life's work." She looks up at me, her blue-green eyes wounded. "I left it to you. I trusted you."

"I know," I say.

"I wanted you to know the truth. I wanted you to have proof."

"It was too much," I say, my voice breaking. "I didn't want to look. By the time I was ready, it was gone. You were gone."

My mother envelops my palm in hers, squeezing it gently.

"You did the best you could," she says. "I know it was too much. It sometimes felt like too much for me." We are both crying.

"I would do things differently now," I say, "but I can't go back in time."

"If only," my mother says. "There are some men I'd like to murder."

"Make sure to leave me your hit list before you go," I say. "I'll see what I can do."

We snort-laugh through our tears.

"I miss you so much, Mom," I say, pulling her into a hug.

"I miss you too, Zenie," she says. "With all of my heart. You are the best thing I ever made. My darling daughter. My girl."

No vows were made or rings exchanged at the Love Party. Instead, we made commitments—to each other; to our children and co-parents; and to our friends, family, and community.

"We commit to witnessing and honouring you in the fullness of who you are as you change and grow," Riley told the people gathered under the tent with us. We stood back to back, leaning against each other as we took turns speaking our commitments into the circle.

"We commit to showing up for you, being in solidarity with you, and sharing our abundance with you," I said.

"We commit to being honest about where we're at, asking for help when we need it, and continuing to grow our ability to move through conflict with care," said Riley.

"We commit to having fun with you, being joyful together, and to continuing to prioritize and tend to our relationships with you," I said. "Always remember that you are the loves of our lives."

Everyone cheered and shouted their well-wishes as Riley and I kissed to seal the spell. Sasha twirled beside us on the grass as she tossed dried wildflower petals into the air.

"I think we just married sixty people," Riley whispered.

"Perfect," I said, reaching for their hand.

Our friend Max, the party's designated jester and bringer of whimsy, doled out kazoos and tambourines to the kids, who led Riley and me in a raucous parade around the circle as people clapped and blew bubbles. (Max also made sure our celebration was well stocked with whoopee cushions, much to the delight of every child there.)

By sunset, we had fed everyone dinner and cupcakes and transformed the tent into a makeshift dance floor. It had been three long pandemic years since I had been at a gay bar. Our backyard party brought back the joy I felt in dancing with other queer people, each moving to our own rhythm as we became a collective body for a night or the length of a song. Riley and I sometimes danced together and sometimes danced apart, always surrounded by friends.

My feet were sore from wearing heels all day by the time the final track of the night, Lizzo's "Everybody's Gay," came on, but I was determined to stretch time by dancing until the very end. The last of us tumbled off the dance floor, hugging and saying our goodbyes as each guest passed through the portal again.

"Guys, you have to see this!" called our friend Casey, beckoning us toward our back door. She was one of several friends staying with us for the weekend.

Two glistening brown slugs were entwined on our stoop in a gooey embrace, their bodies tethered to the concrete by a long white rope of mucus.

"Are they mating?" Riley asked.

"Yeah," said Casey.

The pair of slugs had stowed away in a purple potted hydrangea given to us as a gift. They'd snuck out just in time to close out the Love Party with a sex show.

"Slug sex!" I cried out in delight. "What a blessing."

Riley and I held hands and watched the slugs, marvelling at their oozy undulations. It was hard to tell where one slug ended and the other began. A few feet away, the words *QUEER LOVE IS SACRED AND INFINITE* glittered on the ground.

In *From the Ashes: Grief and Revolution in a World on Fire*, Sarah Jaffe describes grief as "a loss and an opening up simultaneously, an opening up that is terrifying and also necessary." Jaffe writes, "In accepting loss, we make possible the future."[9]

When someone dies, it can feel as if we are outside of chronological time. The lines between past, present, and future become blurry. Memories swirl together with what-ifs, if onlys, and "How will I?" or "How will we?" as we learn to exist in a world where someone we love is gone. Grieving is a process of finding our footing on this unfamiliar landscape. Like memory, it is dynamic, embodied, and relational.

When we grieve, we are remembering the past, but we are also imagining the future. Grieving is a portal; we pass through it and are transformed.

My mother sits beside Corin at our dinner table, with me on her other side. The kids are all talking at once, trying to get their grandmother's attention.

"Grandma Lynne," says Sasha, "look what I made!" She holds up her latest LEGO creation. "It's a magic trick. See?" She reveals its hidden centre.

"Wow!" says my mother.

"I'm a dinosaur," says Corin. "Rawr!"

"I'm a bear," says Alder. "Grrr!"

My mother pretends to be afraid of the fierce creatures at our table.

"Don't eat me!" she says.

"Okay," says Corin.

"Who wants cupcakes?" asks Riley.

"Me! Me! Me!" the kids shout, bouncing in their chairs.

The cupcakes are chocolate with pink icing and rainbow sprinkles. Everyone gets a candle to blow out. Riley passes one each to Sasha, Corin, Alder, Nic, Mars, my mother, and me, then goes around the table lighting the candles, saving the twins' for last.

It's no one's birthday, but we're making up for lost time, so we sing "Happy Birthday" before blowing out the candles. I reach for my mother's hand under the table.

She smiles at me, then looks around as if memorizing our faces. The sunset has tinged the sky through our windows purple-pink. It's almost bedtime. The kids' eyes are getting heavy. I stifle a yawn. "Is it just me or did today feel extra long?"

"It's not just you," she says. "I have to go soon."

"I figured you might. Can I walk you there?"

"I need to do the next part on my own. You know how to find me. A mother doesn't take off into the ether."

"One last thing before you go," I say, beckoning her into the living room.

I sit in the padded grey recliner where I rocked my children to sleep when they were babies. I reach my arms out to my mother. We are awkward at first as we figure out where to place our limbs, but we soon find a comfortable shape as she settles into my lap.

"Is this okay?" she asks, her head resting on my chest.

"More than okay," I say, wrapping myself around her. She relaxes into me as we sway together. I close my eyes, lulled by the rhythm of my mother's breath and my own beating heart.

ACKNOWLEDGMENTS

Thank you to the team at Arsenal Pulp Press for more than fifty years of telling queer stories with courage, integrity, and care: Brian Lam, Robert Ballantyne, Catharine Chen, JC Cham, Cynara Geissler, Erin Chan, and Jazmin Welch.

Thank you to book designer Rebecca Poulin for seeing into the heart of this story.

Thank you to *Xtra Magazine* for publishing the essay that planted the seeds for *Staying Power*, and to Shirarose Wilensky for being the first person to say, "Hey, I think this could be a book."

Thank you to the Canada Council for the Arts for supporting the creation of this work.

Thank you to Ariel Gore and Lidia Yuknavitch for your teaching and mentorship, and for creating writing communities that feel like covens. You've made me a better, braver writer, and I'm grateful for your wisdom, generosity, and encouragement.

I spent hundreds of hours alone at a desk writing *Staying Power*, but it wouldn't exist without the feedback, thought partnership, and support of my friends and writing community. Thank you to Hannah McGregor, Leah Lakshmi Piepzna-Samarasinha, Jen Sookfong Lee, Hil Malatino, Carly Boyce, Megan Linton, Taylor Teal, Joshua Wales, Alex Marzano-Lesnevich, and Kelly Gawel for your feedback on my work-in-progress.

Thank you to Lucie Fielding for thinking with me. Thank you to Shauna Janz for helping me create a sacred container.

Thank you to Hannah McGregor, Leah Lakshmi Piepzna-Samarasinha, and Ariel Gore for your kind words about *Staying Power* and to Jody Chan for letting me use an excerpt from your poem "the garden where our future grows" as the epigraph to this book. I wish I could bend time to give my mother a copy of Jody's book, *impact statement*. Its Mad poetics would have spoken to her own experiences and her survivor-activist's radical care praxis.

Thank you to Jessica Carfagnini, Owen Campbell, and Lukas Maitland for welcoming me into your homes in Thunder Bay and Winnipeg as I was researching *Staying Power*.

Thank you to my friends for celebrating a million deadlines with me, listening to me talk endlessly about this book for two years, and watching *9 to 5* with me. Thank you to my in-laws for the steadfast love and solidarity you have shown me and our family, and for your generosity in giving me (and several of my writer friends) a beautiful space in which to write.

Finally, thank you to my family, whose love, support, and care work made it possible for me to write this book, for trusting me to tell this story and for giving me so many reasons to stay.

NOTES

THE TRAUMA ARCHIVE

1 Lynne Moss Sharman, interview by Wayne Morris, *Mind Control Radio Series*, CKLN 88.1 FM, 2007, transcript at http://members.tranquility.net/~rwinkel/CKLN/HTML2/transc16.htm.

2 Joshua Kendall, "The False Memory Syndrome at 30: How Flawed Science Turned Into Conventional Wisdom," *Mad in America*, February 7, 2021, https://www.madinamerica.com/2021/02/false-memory-syndrome/.

3 Robert Munsch, *Love You Forever* (Firefly Books, 1986).

4 Robert Munsch, "Love You Forever," RobertMunsch.com, accessed April 3, 2025, https://robertmunsch.com/book/love-you-forever.

5 Michelle Caswell et al., *"Come Correct or Don't Come at All": Building More Equitable Relationships Between Archival Studies Scholars and Community Archives*, (UBC/UCLA, 2021), https://escholarship.org/uc/item/7v00k2qz.

AFTER WIFE

1 Stephanie Coontz, *Marriage: A History* (Penguin Books, 2006), Kobo, Introduction.

2 Coontz, *Marriage*, Introduction.

3 Ian Mackenzie, "Who's on First?" *Xtra Magazine*, July 9, 2003, https://xtramagazine.com/power/whos-on-first-43680.

4 Philippe de Montigny, "Still Fighting," *CBC News*, June 10, 2023, https://www.cbc.ca/newsinteractives/features/same-sex-marriage-canada-lgbtq.

5 Tracy Tyler, "Spouse Ruling Allows First Gay Divorce," *Toronto Star*, September 14, 2004.

6 Tyler, "Spouse Ruling."

7 Brenda Cossman, "Getting Unmarried: Same-Sex Couples Need the Exit Option," *Globe and Mail*, September 16, 2004, https://www.law.utoronto.ca/news/article-cossman-same-sex-divorce.

8 Cossman, "Getting Unmarried."

9 Tyler, "Spouse Ruling."

10 Colin Campbell, "Gay Pair Seeks Canada's First Same-Sex Divorce," *New York Times*, July 22, 2004.

11 de Montigny, "Still Fighting."

12 Gina Cherelus, "Shared Pain: A Breakup Unsettles a Couple's Fans," *New York Times*, March 28, 2024.

13 Laya Neelakandan, "Why This Queer South Asian Couple's Breakup Is 'Devastating' for Their Fans," *Today*, March 27, 2024, https://www.today.com/popculture/news/anjali-chakra-sufi-malik-breakup-explained-rcna145211.

14 Samantha Grindell, "A Same-Sex Couple Took Stunning Anniversary Photos That Show Them Wearing Traditional South Asian Clothes," *Business Insider*, August 13, 2020, https://www.businessinsider.com/same-sex-couple-took-pictures-in-traditional-south-asian-clothes-2019-12.

15 Abby Monteil, "This Queer Influencer Couple's Cheating Drama Has Taken Over TikTok. Here's What Happened," *them*, March 26, 2024, https://www.them.us/story/anjali-chakra-sufi-malik-breakup-wedding.

16 Neelakandan, "Couple's Breakup."

17 Anjali Chakra (@anjalichakra), "hi loves this is part 1 of my breakup recovery series," Instagram reel, August 1, 2024,

https://www.instagram.com/reel/C-IhVHSJRcL/?igsh=MWdoMjlvNmZhNXl6dA==.

18 Kayla Kumari Upadhyaya, "The Anjali Chakra x Sufi Malik Breakup and Cheating Confession, Explained," *Autostraddle*, March 25, 2024, https://www.autostraddle.com/anjali-chakra-sufi-malik-breakup-and-cheating-explained/.

19 Abigail Ocobock, *Marriage Material: How an Enduring Institution Is Changing Same-Sex Relationships* (University of Chicago Press, 2024), 20.

20 Ocobock, *Marriage Material*, 15.

21 Ocobock, *Marriage Material*, 15.

22 Katrina Kimport, *Queering Marriage: Challenging Family Formation in the United States* (Rutgers University Press, 2014).

23 US General Accounting Office, *Defense of Marriage Act: Update to Prior Report* (US General Accounting Office, 2004), http://www.gao.gov/new.items/d04353r.pdf.

24 Vincent Francoeur, host, *Mental Health Much?*, podcast, "Gay Divorce," July 6, 2024, https://creators.spotify.com/pod/profile/vincent-francoeur9/episodes/E-71---Gay-Divorce-e2lhhpu.

25 Marie-Amélie George, *Family Matters: Queer Households and the Half-Century Struggle for Legal Recognition* (Cambridge University Press, 2024), 265.

26 Gabrielle Emanuel, "How Making History Unmade a Family," *NPR*, May 16, 2019, https://www.npr.org/2019/05/16/723647834/how-making-history-unmade-a-family.

27 Emanuel, "Making History."

28 Emanuel, "Making History."

29 Emanuel, "Making History."

30 Ocobock, *Marriage Material*, 153.

LEARNING TO STAY

1 Gaston Bachelard, *The Poetics of Space* (Penguin Books, 2014), Kobo, Chapter 9.
2 Julietta Singh, *The Breaks* (Coffee House Books, 2021), 48–49.
3 Singh, *The Breaks*, 49.
4 Singh, *The Breaks*, 51.
5 Singh, *The Breaks*, 48.

BEST INTERESTS OF THE CHILD

1 Minnie Bruce Pratt, "One Good Mother to Another: Lesbian Mothers Fight for Custody of Children," *The Progressive*, November 1993, https://www.glapn.org/sodomylaws/usa/virginia/vanews25.htm.
2 John Hammontree, "Minnie Bruce Pratt on Being Targeted by Anti-LGBTQ Laws in North Carolina," *Reckon*, April 22, 2021, https://www.reckon.news/podcast/2021/04/minnie-bruce-pratt-on-being-targeted-by-anti-lgbtq-laws-in-north-carolina.html.
3 Minnie Bruce Pratt, *S/He* (Alyson Books, 1995), 43.
4 Daniel Winunwe Rivers, *Radical Relations: Lesbian Mothers, Gay Fathers, and Their Children in the United States Since World War II* (University of North Carolina Press, 2013), Kobo, Chapter 3.
5 Marie-Amélie George, *Family Matters: Queer Households and the Half-Century Struggle for Legal Recognition* (Cambridge University Press, 2024), 7.
6 George, *Family Matters*, 32.
7 Rivers, *Radical Relations*, Chapter 3.
8 Erin Gallagher-Cohoon, *Queerly Familial: Canadian Histories of Queer Reproduction, Parenting, and Activism, 1968–2005* (PhD thesis, Queen's University, 2024), 33, https://qspace.library.queensu.ca/items/8bb6e3dd-2d23-4c79-9185-ac5322b50111.

9 Halnya Freeland, "Custody Rights for the Nonconformist," *Branching Out* V, no. 1 (1978): 5.

10 Katherine Arnup, *Lesbian Parenting: Living with Pride and Prejudice* (Gynergy Books, 1995), 382.

11 Minnie Bruce Pratt, "The Struggle to Write," *Poetry Foundation*, December 13, 2011, https://www.poetryfoundation.org/articles/69759/the-struggle-to-write.

12 Minnie Bruce Pratt, *Crime Against Nature* (Sinister Wisdom, 2013), 119.

13 Julie Enzer, introduction to *Crime Against Nature*, by Minnie Bruce Pratt (Sinister Wisdom, 2013), 17.

14 Amanda Holpuch, "The Supreme Court Struck Down Sodomy Laws 20 Years Ago. Some Still Remain," *New York Times*, July 21, 2023.

15 Pratt, *Crime Against Nature*, 137.

16 Hammontree, "Minnie Bruce Pratt."

17 Jason Proctor, "B.C. Judge Orders Second Mother Declared a Third Parent to Child of Polyamorous Trio," CBC *News*, April 26, 2021, https://www.cbc.ca/news/canada/british-columbia/polyamorous-parents-birth-certificate-judge-1.6002991.

18 Rivers, *Radical Relations*, Chapter 7.

19 Sarah Matthiesen, *Reproduction Reconceived: Family Making and the Limits of Choice After Roe v. Wade* (University of California Press, 2021), Kobo, Chapter 1.

20 Katie Batza, "From Sperm Runners to Sperm Banks: Lesbians, Assisted Conception, and Challenging the Fertility Industry, 1971–1983," *Journal of Women's History 28*, no. 2 (2016), 84.

21 Matthiesen, *Reproduction Reconceived*, Chapter 1.

22 Shulamith Firestone, *The Dialectic of Sex: The Case for Feminist Revolution* (William Morrow and Company, 1970), 206.

23 Gay Liberation Front, *Gay Liberation Front Manifesto* (Gay Liberation Front, 1971), 15.

24 Rivers, *Radical Relations*, Chapter 6; Gallagher-Cohoon, *Queerly Familial*, 222.
25 Batza, "Sperm Runners."
26 Rivers, *Radical Relations*, Chapter 7.
27 Jane Severance, *Lots of Mommies* (Lollipop Power, 1983), 18, archived at https://archive.org/details/lots-of-mommies-by-jane-severance/mode/2up.
28 Severance, *Lots of Mommies*, 32.
29 Thomas Crisp, "Setting the Record 'Straight': An Interview with Jane Severance," *Children's Literature Association Quarterly* 35, no. 1 (2010), 94.
30 Crisp, "Record 'Straight.'"
31 Rivers, *Radical Relations*, Chapter 5.
32 Rivers, *Radical Relations*, Chapter 5.
33 Rivers, *Radical Relations*, Chapter 5.
34 Rivers, *Radical Relations*, Chapter 5.
35 George, *Family Matters*, 265.
36 Sandra Patton-Imani, *Queering Family Trees: Race, Reproductive Justice, and Lesbian Motherhood* (NYU Press, 2020), Kobo, Chapter 5.
37 Patton-Imani, *Queering Family Trees*, Chapter 5.
38 Catherine Opie, "Drag, Gridiron and Kids in Tutus: America Through the Lens of Catherine Opie—In Pictures," *The Guardian*, April 16, 2023, https://www.theguardian.com/artanddesign/gallery/2023/apr/17/drag-gridiron-and-kids-in-tutus-america-through-the-lens-of-catherine-opie-in-pictures.
39 Nat Trotman and Jennifer Blessing, *Catherine Opie: American Photographer* (Guggenheim Museum, 2008), 16.
40 Trotman and Blessing, *Catherine Opie*, 258.
41 Maggie Nelson, *The Argonauts* (Graywolf Press, 2015), 64.
42 Trotman and Blessing, *Catherine Opie*, 258.

43 Dorothy Allison, “The Story of Art: Catherine Opie’s Eye,” in *Catherine Opie: American Photographer*, edited by Nat Trotman and Jennifer Blessing (Guggenheim Museum, 2008), 269.
44 Allison, “Story of Art,” 269.
45 Dorothy Allison, “I Never Believed in the Perfect Mother,” *Southern Cultures 22*, no. 3 (2016), https://www.southerncultures.org/article/never-believed-perfect-mother/.
46 Allison, “Story of Art,” 269.
47 George, *Family Matters*, 77.
48 Gallagher-Cohoon, *Queerly Familial*, 58.
49 Gallagher-Cohoon, *Queerly Familial*, 62.
50 George, *Family Matters*, 77.
51 Gallagher-Cohoon, *Queerly Familial*, 89.
52 George, *Family Matters*, 261.
53 George, *Family Matters*, 265.

DOLLY, DORALEE, MY MOTHER, AND ME

1 “Domestic Box Office for 1980,” Box Office Mojo by IMDbPro, accessed May 29, 2025, https://www.boxofficemojo.com/year/1980/.
2 SC Dillon (@scdamndillon), “A butch will help you move,” Twitter, January 28, 2021.
3 Marianela D’Aprile, “9to5 Brought Women Into Labor and Working-Class Women Into the Women’s Movement,” *Jacobin*, February 1, 2021, https://jacobin.com/2021/02/9to5-labor-working-class-womens-movement-karen-nussbaum.
4 Ellen Cassedy, *Working 9 to 5: A Women’s Movement, a Labor Union, and the Iconic Movie* (Chicago Review Press, 2023), Kobo, Chapter 13.
5 Cassedy, *Working 9 to 5*, Chapter 13.

6 Jad Abumrad, host, *Dolly Parton's America*, podcast, season 1, episode 5, "Dollitics," WNYC Studios, November 12, 2019, https://www.wnycstudios.org/podcasts/dolly-partons-america/episodes/dollitics?tab=transcript.

7 Abumrad, "Dollitics."

8 Abumrad, "Dollitics."

9 Roger Ebert, "*Nine to Five*: Review," December 19, 1980, https://www.rogerebert.com/reviews/nine-to-five-1980.

10 Tressie McMillan Cottom, "The Dolly Moment: Why We Stan a Post-Racism Queen," *essaying*, February 24, 2021, https://tressie.substack.com/p/the-dolly-moment.

11 Dolly Parton, *Dolly: My Life and Other Unfinished Business* (HarperCollins, 1994), 202.

12 Parton, *Dolly*, 204.

13 Sarah Smarsh, *She Come By It Natural: Dolly Parton and the Women Who Lived Her Songs* (Scribner, 2020), 4.

14 Smarsh, *She Come By It*, 4.

15 Steacy Easton, *Dolly Parton's White Limozeen* (Bloomsbury Publishing, 2024), Kobo, Introduction.

16 McMillan Cottom, "Dolly Moment."

(M)OTHER

1 Amanda Brennan, "Abortion Rights and the Eugenic and Racist Origins of Having It All," *Nursing Clio*, May 10, 2022, https://nursingclio.org/2022/05/10/abortion-rights-and-the-eugenic-and-racist-origins-of-having-it-all/.

2 Jennifer Szalai, "The Complicated Origins of 'Having It All,'" *New York Times Magazine*, January 2, 2015, https://www.nytimes.com/2015/01/04/magazine/the-complicated-origins-of-having-it-all.html.

3 Helen Gurley Brown, *Having It All: Love, Success, Sex, Money, Even If You're Starting with Nothing* (Pocket Books, 1982), 66.

4 Leah Lakshmi Piepzna-Samarasinha, *Care Work: Dreaming Disability Justice* (Arsenal Pulp Press, 2018), 218.

5 Jenny Fran Davis, "Mean Mommies: Care in Contemporary Queer Literature," *Los Angeles Review of Books*, November 27, 2024, https://lareviewofbooks.org/article/mean-mommies-care-in-contemporary-queer-literature/.

6 Mistress Danielle Blunt, "Mommy Dommes and Caregiver Archetypes: An Interview with Jessie Sage," *Mistress Blunt*, March 4, 2021, https://www.mistressblunt.com/mommy-dommes-and-caregiver-archetypes-an-interview-with-jessie-sage/.

7 Blunt, "Mommy Dommes."

LOVE ME BACK TO LIFE

1 Bridget Murray, "What Makes Mental Time Travel Possible?" *Monitor on Psychology 34*, no. 9 (2003), accessed February 2, 2025, https://www.apa.org/monitor/oct03/mental.

2 Endel Tulving, "Chronesthesia: Conscious Awareness of Subjective Time," in *Principles of Frontal Lobe Function*, eds. Donald T. Stuss and Robert T. Knight (Oxford Academic, 2002), 311.

3 Jerome Groopman, "Can Forgetting Help You Remember?" *The New Yorker*, May 13, 2024, https://www.newyorker.com/magazine/2024/05/20/why-we-remember-charan-ranganath-book-review.

4 Mary-Frances O'Connor, *The Grieving Brain: The Surprising Science of How We Learn from Love and Loss* (HarperOne, 2022), Kobo, Chapter 10.

5 Matthew Ratcliffe, Louise Richardson, and Becky Millar, "On the Appropriateness of Grief to Its Object," *Journal of the American Philosophical Association* 9, no. 2 (2023), 331–332.

6 Christopher McCarroll and Karen Yan, "Mourning a Death Foretold: Memory and Mental Time Travel in Anticipatory Grief," *Phenomenology and the Cognitive Sciences* (2024), https://doi.org/10.1007/s11097-024-09956-z.

7 Donald J. Robinaugh and Richard J. McNally, "Remembering the Past and Envisioning the Future in Bereaved Adults With and Without Complicated Grief," *Clinical Psychological Science* 1, no. 3 (2013), 298.

8 Justina Pociunaite and Tabea Wolf, "I Will Keep Your Memory! Reasons for Remembering Lost Loved Ones," *Applied Cognitive Psychology* 37 (2023), 1404.

9 Sarah Jaffe, *From the Ashes: Grief and Revolution in a World on Fire* (Bold Type Books, 2024), Kobo, Introduction.

Photo by Jamie-Leigh Gonzales

ZENA SHARMAN is an essayist and non-fiction writer whose work explores themes of community, identity, and care. She is the editor of several anthologies, including *The Care We Dream Of: Liberatory & Transformative Approaches to LGBTQ+ Health* (Arsenal Pulp Press, 2021) and Lambda Literary Award–winning *The Remedy: Queer and Trans Voices on Health and Health Care* (Arsenal Pulp Press, 2016). Zena co-edited *Persistence: All Ways Butch and Femme* (Arsenal Pulp Press, 2011), which was named a Stonewall Honor Book and nominated for a Lambda Literary Award. *Staying Power* is her debut memoir. ***zenasharman.com***